A STUDENT'S GUIDE TO COLLEGE SUCCESS

Personal Safety, Relationships, and Transitions

Koreem R. Bell and Carol K. Rothera

cognella® | ACADEMIC PUBLISHING

Bassim Hamadeh, CEO and Publisher
Kassie Graves, Acquisitions Editor
Leah Sheets, Project Editor
Berenice Quirino, Associate Production Editor
Miguel Macias, Senior Graphic Designer
Alexa Lucido, Licensing Associate
Don Kesner, Interior Designer
Natalie Piccotti, Director of Marketing
Kassie Graves, Vice President of Editorial
Jamie Giganti, Director of Academic Publishing

Cover: Copyright © 2017 iStockphoto LP/DGLimages.

Printed in the United States of America.

ISBN: 978-1-5165-1672-8 (pbk)

cognella® | ACADEMIC PUBLISHING

A STUDENT'S GUIDE TO COLLEGE SUCCESS

THE COGNELLA SERIES ON STUDENT SUCCESS

S tudent success isn't always measured in straight As.

Many students arrive at college believing that if they study hard and earn top grades, their higher education experience will be a success. Few recognize that some of their greatest learning opportunities will take place outside the classroom. Learning how to manage stress, navigate new relationships, or put together a budget can be just as important as acing a pop quiz.

The Cognella Series on Student Success is a collection of books designed to help students develop the essential life and learning skills needed to support a happy, healthy, and productive higher education experience. Featuring topics suggested by students and books written by experts, the series offers research-based, yet practical advice to help any student navigate new challenges and succeed throughout their college experience.

Series Editor: Richard Parsons, Ph.D.
Professor of Counselor Education, West Chester University

Other titles available in the series:

- *A Student's Guide to Stress Management*
- *A Student's Guide to a Meaningful Career*
- *A Student's Guide to Self-Care*
- *A Student's Guide to Money Matters*
- *A Student's Guide to Self-Presentation*
- *A Student's Guide to Exercise for Improving Health*
- *A Student's Guide to College Transition*
- *A Student's Guide to Math Success*

ABOUT THE AUTHORS

T he transition to college is full of new and exciting opportunities! But with those opportunities also comes significant change. Living away from friends and family, making new connections, ensuring your personal safety, and making healthy decisions are just a few of the challenges you'll face as you transition to college life.

A Student's Guide to College Success: Personal Safety, Relationships, and Transitions provides you with all the practical advice you'll need to address the physical, social, and psychological challenges associated with becoming a college student. In this guide, you'll learn basic skills for living on your own, managing your money, asserting yourself, establishing boundaries, and keeping yourself safe in new social situations.

This guide will help you approach your new college lifestyle with confidence, self-awareness, and the tools you need to take care of yourself and succeed throughout your college career.

A Student's Guide to College Success is part of the Cognella Series on Student Success, a collection of books designed to help students develop the essential life and learning skills needed to support a happy, healthy, and productive higher education experience.

Koreem R. Bell is an adjunct professor of counselor education at West Chester University, and a school counselor for the West Chester Area School District.

Carol K. Rothera is currently the supervisor of Student Services for the West Chester Area School District and an adjunct professor in counselor education department at West Chester University. She was an intervention specialist for 20 years.

BRIEF CONTENTS

DETAILED CONTENTS

EDITOR'S PREFACE

The transition to college marks a significant milestone in a person's life. Many of you will be preparing to live away from your friends and family for the very first time. Clearly this is and should be an exciting time.

It is a time to experience new things and experiment with new options. While the opportunity to grow is clear—so too are the many challenges you are to experience as you transition from high school to college.

Research suggests that the first year of college is the most difficult period of adjustment a student faces. Not only will you be required to adjust to new academic demands, but you will also have to navigate a number of social and emotional challenges that accompany your life as a college student. The books found within this series—*Cognella Series on Student Success*—have been developed to help you with the many issues confronting your successful transition from life as a high school student to life as a collegiate. Each book within the series was designed to provide research-based yet *practical* advice to assist you succeeding in your college experience.

The current book, *A Student's Guide to College Life and Changing Relationships,* by Koreem Bell and Carol Rothera provides you with well-researched, practical advice in addressing the physical, social, and psychological threats to personal safety that one can encounter transitioning to this new college environment. The authors, in their preface, note that the dropout rate from colleges and universities in the United States is 40 percent. While it can be assumed that many of these students simply did not have the academic skills necessary for success, the sad reality is that many drop out because of their inability to adapt to the social and emotional demands encountered in this new environment. Many students find it difficult to cope with experiences such as separating from old friends and family; making new social connections; handling the expanded independence and the need to make healthy decisions, often on your own, and as a result make the decision to withdraw from college.

Your entry into college marks a major life change for you and your parents. The information you will find in this book will help you to experience college as enjoyable and life enriching.

While the topic is certainly serious and the information presented comes from well-researched sources, the book is both practical and engaging. The book employs case illustrations in a feature called "*Voices From Campus*" and opportunities to apply what you are learning in a feature called "*Your Turn.*"

This is an exciting time for you. It is also a time of challenge. But with the information provided within this book, as well as the other books within the series, I know you will be able to meet the challenge, embrace the experience, and make a successful transition from high school to college.

Richard Parsons, Ph.D.
Series Editor

AUTHORS' PREFACE

O ne of the joys of working in a high school setting is seeing our students finally graduate after 13 years of formal education. We are the privileged educators that are able to reap the rewards of the herculean efforts of dozens of our colleagues, culminating in that final walk down the graduation aisle to receive a well-deserved high school diploma. We are well aware that the joy that emanates from those students and their families was not just our doing, but the result of a village of people: teachers, staff, and administrators, working together to prepare their students for the adventure that lies ahead. *Then*, after they leave *us*, we begin to ask the same questions that may have run through the minds of our elementary and middle school colleagues. We hope that wherever our former students may reside and whatever it is that they are doing, that they are safe and happy. Sometimes, if we are fortunate, students return to their old high school after their first break, or at seemingly random times. Some want to visit the favorite teacher that inspired them, others want to see the principal who motivated them, and some just want to hear the words of wisdom that the security greeter bestowed upon them when they felt down. But when they visit their *school counselor*, it could be for any number of reasons. The majority of our visits involve students wanting to transfer from one college to another due to an incident that occurred or because it was not a "good fit" for them. Or they are having trouble dealing with problems that the counselor helped them through when they were students, and want to seek our guidance once again. As veteran counselors with 40 years of combined experience, we have heard many stories about what happens once students leave our doors and why they come back to us after experiencing difficulty. When the series editor offered us an opportunity to write a book about how students can better prepare themselves for the challenges that await after high school, we became very excited to share some of those stories with you.

We are particularly enthusiastic about this book's premise because we feel that there is much emphasis given to preparing parents and students *academically* for college, but not enough attention is devoted to the social and emotional barriers to student success. We hope that this book can be used both as a guide and workbook to prepare parents and high school seniors for the unspoken things that are ignored until they become a personal issue. Each chapter contains an activity that can be done together or individually, along with real world examples that our past students have faced over the years. Issues related to the use and abuse of drugs and alcohol, lack of time management, financial unpreparedness, and social awareness are more responsible for students dropping out or transferring than any other reason. Telling a student to go to college and do well is not enough. We need to make sure that they are as ready as possible for college before they leave the security and safety of their home environment. We believe that if our high school graduates are well-equipped in every possible area, we can eliminate some of the factors that lead to their lack of success.

As we were preparing to write this preface, a former student visited our office, dejected. It turns out that she had to leave her college for financial reasons, and her hopes of returning for her second semester were bleak. After hearing the complete backstory and making some phone calls, the former student was able to start classes the following week at our local community college. I praised the student for seeking out our help, but then I wondered how many former students are in her situation but do not ever ask for help? We are hoping that this book will empower students and their parents to take a proactive role in ensuring that preventable situations are recognized and addressed before the students move into their college residence halls. As much as we want to see our former students return, if we could cut down on the surprise visits in exchange for empowering students now with the ways and means to prevent future hardship, we would feel that is a worthwhile trade-off! The process of completing this book has helped us become better informed as counselor-educators, which has already benefited the students that we work with daily. We hope that this book has the same effect on you and your family.

OVERVIEW

Finally! After many months of preparation and implementation, all of your college applications are submitted, your teachers have sent your letters of recommendation, and your school counselor has *assured* you that your transcript has been sent. You have no doubt in your mind that you have worked your tail off to find the college that is the best fit for you. Everything is finished!! Time to relax, right? Not! Getting accepted to a college is only the *first* part of the journey towards completing a four-year degree. The hard work to become a successful, independent human being has just begun. For you and your parents, the remainder of the school year should be filled with transition tasks or goals to prepare you for one of the biggest challenges of your life.

So many parents feel as if their students are ready to make these huge decisions on their own. They have done well so far, right? Our students can handle it—their grades are good, they have an active social life, they manage their time wisely—senior year should be a breeze!

The reality is that your student has been in the same school for the past four years and now has a firm grasp on how the *high school* system operates. They have developed an academic protocol and have formed close friendships with their peers. All this has been accomplished with most of their basic needs met and little or no financial responsibilities. So . . . are they really ready??? The dropout rate from colleges and universities in the United States is 40 percent. The top reason for this dropout rate is because students are not able to balance all of the new changes introduced into their lives. Students withdraw from school not only because of academics or lack of intelligence, but also (and most frequently) due to social and emotional issues which have accumulated during their first year of college. Sometimes students lack the coping skills/strategies or planning abilities necessary to rebound when they are faced with a number of challenges and struggles. Parents and students usually don't spend enough time preparing for this critical transitional period. Very little effort is devoted to preparing students for major life changes, which can leave students dejected and feeling like failures. When this happens, students become overwhelmed and isolated without the support that has always been there, causing them to return *home*. It is our hope that this book will provide you with the information needed to prepare you and your family for these obstacles and will equip you with tools necessary to plan for and guarantee a productive and successful college experience.

A Student's Guide to College Life and Changing Relationships
Koreem R. Bell, Ed.D., & Carol Rothera, M.S.
West Chester University, West Chester Area School District

EMOTIONAL ROLLERCOASTER

Over the decades, we have heard this same story over and over . . . "My senior must have a serious problem. One minute they are cuddling with me, and the next minute they are fighting me because of some silly task that I asked them to complete!" You may question yourself, asking "Where did I go wrong raising my student?" or "I really can't believe this is my kid." Both you and your student could be experiencing a variety of emotions, ranging anywhere from excitement to fear, and from pride to anxiety. Senior year is a stressful time for any student, and is filled with many milestones and achievements. It can be compared in many ways to the first year of life. For example, that we learned to crawl then walk, make sounds, then talk, and all of these things happened in a short period of time, creating the need for families to make many adjustments and adaptations in their home life.

It's possible that a similar thing could be happening now. While they aren't bumping into furniture and making unintelligible noises, your student may be pushing away from you in order to master and test out their future independence to prove to everyone that they are ready for adult responsibilities. Family members and friends are constantly asking if they are ready for college and all of the big, exciting changes that are forthcoming, and lamenting about how different college is from the "real world." After all, they are almost 18, so that means they must be ready for life's challenges, right? Take Donna for example, who wanted to attend college in a setting very different from the one in which she grew up (Voices From Campus 1.1).

VOICES FROM CAMPUS 1.1

Donna

I was so excited about going to college. I chose to go to a large college in an urban setting very different from my small suburban upbringing. I wanted the exposure of what a city had to offer—lots of culture and entertainment. This was very different than my boring, peaceful country-like setting. I felt college was an opportunity to experience things outside my comfort zone and to get a feel for what it is like in the real world. At that time, that's what I was hearing from everyone around me. College is the time to spread your wings.

Looking back on my senior year in high school, I was a bit nervous. Many people were asking where I had decided to go to college. When I told them the name of the university, their response was not what I expected. Frequently the reaction was "That's a great college but it is not in the best part of the city. How are you going to handle that? You better be careful. How do you parents feel about that choice?" I was told stories of people getting mugged and chased. But I also heard about how great it was to go the museums and cultural events that I could never experience in a rural setting. I almost changed my original choice of colleges because of what others were saying. I felt I was giving in to my fears.

All these remarks created lots of stress and confusion. At the time I was trying to get through the end of my senior year and was distracted by all of the thoughts going through my head. I even found myself not sleeping well, which made me cranky and moody. I could not believe that I had questioned my choice of universities. I worked so hard to make sure it was a perfect fit for me. My parents had already put money down and I had a roommate that seemed great.

I was lucky because my sister's best friend went to the same university. I set up a time to talk with her about her experience at college. She acknowledged that the university was not in the best location, but she said understanding where you can go and where you should not go is really important. She did not have any problems the years she attended there. Just like me she had a great experience and loved what she learned about different kinds of people in our world and what she learned about herself. I can't believe I almost withdrew my application.

It may look like they are not in need of assistance, guidance or support, especially since they tell you exactly that over and over again. But students do need safe environments to experiment with this new thing called *independence*.

Additionally, your student, in an effort to form their own identity, is beginning to question the morals and values that you have instilled in them to determine if they will adopt them as their own. The possibility that they may need to be separate from you in order to move towards that growth is very real, and can also be very scary.

Another emotional milestone quickly approaching is the loss of lifelong friendships. Many students that have lived in the same area for their entire lives and have friends they have known for that long are facing the prospect of never seeing them again after high school. Going away to college will change these close relationships in ways they do not yet realize. Students usually react to this in a couple of different ways. One way they do this is by pulling away from their friends in order to make the loss process less painful, another example is becoming super close to their friends in order to hold on to those relationships for as long as they can before they leave high school. These reactions can cause conflicts with longtime childhood friends, which are sometimes petty and fleeting, but hurtful nonetheless. Hurt and emotionally distressed relationships are usually the result of students using this protective mechanism.

Parents also go through their own emotional trepidations during this time. As they start to realize that their student will be moving away to a new environment, it dawns on them that they will not be able to readily assist their student if something goes wrong. As parents, you will no longer have control over what they are eating, when they are sleeping, or what they are doing at any given time. And you *know* that something will go wrong, it has to at some point—that's a part of life. This is the time to test your skills as a parent. Ask yourself: Have you prepared your student for these life challenges? Will they be safe? Will they listen to your words of wisdom? Are *you* prepared??? So what *can* you do? Consider the activity suggested in Your Turn 1.1 as a step that can help maintain your bond, your *connection* to your student, during this period of transition.

YOUR TURN 1.1

Bonding Activity

Directions: Set up a designated time to meet with your student, at least twice a month, in a relaxed atmosphere. Make it a place you both enjoy outside of your home. It could be a favorite place to eat or an activity that you both enjoy. Set goals to accomplish. Openly share your thoughts and encourage your student to discuss theirs as well. This will promote an open communication between the both of you. It will also help you better understand what your student is currently experiencing. Also, it will better help your student understand where you are coming from. As you reinforce your bonds as parent and student, it will be easier to set up a plan to determine what the both of you can do to get them ready to start college, well-equipped.

Question	Parent Response	Student Response	Prevention Plan
What do you think will be the most fun in college? Could this become a problem?			
If a problem arises in college, do you think that you can advocate (speak up) for yourself?			
What do think will be the most challenging part of being away from home?			
What will be the most challenging part of your social life?			
What are your worries about college?			
What do you think are possible dangers of being in a college environment?			

This family activity will help you and your student navigate senior year and the first year of college. This level of communication is vital in order to monitor and support your student's well-being.

We can appreciate that sometimes our emerging adults do not necessarily value our words of wisdom. It may be useful to engage the help of others who more closely speak their language. This person could be a relative, neighbor, or family friend that has gone through a collegiate experience recent enough to provide added listening value to your student. Your Turn 1.2 invites you to elicit the help and the perspective of someone who has recently navigated their first year of college.

YOUR TURN 1.2

Learning from the Experiences of Others: Questions for a Current College Student

During one of these planned get-togethers, you could invite a recent college sophomore or junior. Ask them how they felt during their first year in college. It can be helpful to hear the struggles from a person close to your student's age. In their eyes you may seem to be too old to understand what college is like now. Hearing a current college student's viewpoint could help to reinforce many of the things you have been saying.

Question	Does this affect me?	Prevention Plan (What can I do?)
What were the highs and lows of your first year? What could you have done differently to prepare for the experience?		
What was your first month of college like?		
What was the hardest adjustment for you?		
Were you ever homesick? What did you do to feel better?		
What was it like to be totally independent and have no one to answer to?		

Question	Does this affect me?	Prevention Plan (What can I do?)
How did you manage your social life?		
Did you have any worries? What were they?		
What are the campus rules about drug/alcohol use? What happens if they aren't followed?		
Did you have a roommate your first year? Did you get along with them? If not, what happened?		

Other ways to invite conversation and increase the helpful bond might be to participate in activities outside of the home. These can be great opportunities to bring up sensitive topics like drug and alcohol use, sex, and safety—not necessarily to preach to them about what they should or should not do, but to discuss what they could be faced with and how to remain safe and protected. Statistics about students being kicked out of college due to underage drinking or the prevalence of date rape should be discussed as preventative measures and taken seriously. These issues are real and should be addressed before students leave for the college, as they will have to make many decisions on their own using the experiences and skills they have gained so far.

If these conversations get too overwhelming or things get to the point where you or your student just cannot have a productive conversation, additional support may be needed. It is not unusual for a senior in high school to seek counseling by a trained professional. Numerous things are changing in their lives, and with that, an increase in stress is typical. All of us deal differently with stress and change. Having someone who is not emotionally or personally involved and who can listen to and process all the questions that may arise can be very beneficial. Therapists can help set goals and strategies to work with a student and/or family to provide direction and purpose in the transition process.

1.1: The Take Away

We hope that you take the following away from this chapter:

- Getting accepted into college is only the first step in the preparation process for a successful college experience.

- Understanding and planning for the social and emotional aspects of college life are as important as the academics.

- The parent and student relationship experiences many emotional ups and downs during senior year before college.

- Exploring and planning for the challenges may reduce the feeling of being overwhelmed and can potentially reduce the dropout rates for college.

IT'S SO HARD TO SAY GOODBYE TO YESTERDAY

O ver the years, we have watched thousands of seniors run the last lap of their high school race; inevitably, at some point reality strikes them and they realize that every passing moment with their teachers and friends will soon come to an end. As we reflected on this, a famous tune, originally written by Freddie Perren and Christine Yarian in 1975 but made popular by the R&B group Boyz II Men in the 1990s, comes to mind. The song, *It's So Hard to Say Goodbye to Yesterday*, does a wonderful job of encapsulating all the amazing (and sometimes tumultuous) experiences that high school students endure over the course of four years. The seemingly infinite amount of nights and weekends to hang out with friends suddenly has an *end date*, and feelings of excitement begin to blur with sadness as the march towards graduation trudges on. If you have never heard the song before, stop reading this book *right now* and listen to it. It's okay—we'll wait!

As students, we tend to think, "How could I be so lucky to have so many close friends in one place?" Eventually as you mature, you begin to realize that, while your friends were awesome and fun to hang out with, the main reason that you were close with them is because of the proximity you had to each other. You will wonder about all of the people that you could one day meet who are *not* in your neighborhood, school, sports team, or hometown! This prospect is exciting to some and terrifying to others.

In high school, it can be very easy as a senior to believe that the friends you have, the ones that have been with you since kindergarten, will always be around, no matter what, for your entire life. However, graduation day arrives, and just like that . . . your companions are gone. The people that you played, laughed, cried, complained, studied, and hung out with have moved on, each going their separate path. Sure, there will be the occasional get-together during Thanksgiving and holiday break, as well as the class re-unions five, ten, twenty, etcetera, etcetera years down the line, but ultimately the friendships as you knew them will be forever altered. Even though your friends are still out there in the world, not being able to see them daily in class, lunch, or study hall can be a tough pill to swallow. Sure, you will try to keep in touch, either by texting, following or liking their posts in the latest social media apps, or maybe even by (gasp!) calling them by phone. But you may find out that it doesn't have that same feel as seeing them in person.

No student will respond to these changes in the same way. Take Zhané, for example, a student that wasn't as concerned about the classmates she would leave behind, but rather the family and teacher relationships (Voices From Campus 2.1).

VOICES FROM CAMPUS 2.1

Zhané

I first visited my college as a high school sophomore on a field trip with my school. When I got off the bus and arrived on campus, I knew it was the place for me; the people were friendly, there was a band playing as we got off the bus, and a dance team was performing in the auditorium as we entered and waited for the presentation. And I even got to meet and take a picture with the homecoming king! After that trip, I knew that I had to go there.

Fast-forward two years later, and it's time for me to apply to college! My tenth grade *fave* was still my number one choice. I re-member that it was March of my senior year when I read a letter from the fave college stating that I was accepted. I was *beyond* excited! But my joy immediately turned to fear because I started worrying about my family. My mom is a single parent, and I help her out a lot, and I'm *kind of* almost like a second parent. Thankfully, I am not far away from home (about 45 minutes), and I can return home to help out if my mom really needs me. Otherwise, I come home on the weekends a lot to work, and sometimes during the weekdays that I don't have class.

I also was worried about how I was going to pay for college. Fortunately, I received some scholarship money from my school, and financial aid covered the rest. Also, I still work at a local grocery store on weekends and on breaks to pay for my phone and gas for my car.

Truthfully, I don't really miss the people I graduated with. We didn't really get along. I was friendlier with people that were already gone and in college than with the people in school with me. The ones that I do miss I make time to see on breaks. We go out for lunch, to the movies, or things like that.

Also, I spent a lot of time with my teachers, especially the culinary teacher and my counselor. When it was almost graduation time, I went to visit every teacher that I ever had here to say goodbye. They always gave me help and support, and they really seemed to care about me and my well-being. My culinary teacher still asks me to stop by to show the new students how to make sugar cookies. She said that I was the standard that they have to live up to! That's why I go back to my high school whenever I can.

As you transition into the next phase of your life, it is helpful to take time to review the good, the bad, and the ugly of what has gone before (see Your Turn 2.1).

YOUR TURN 2.1

High School—Four Years in Review

Directions: There are going to be many aspects of high school that you will miss, whether you realize it now or not. Whether the experiences were fun

(Homecoming! Prom!) or excruciatingly painful (accounting class—yuck!), these moments helped to shape who you are. The following questions serve as prompts to help you think about the highs and lows over the course of your high school career. Think carefully about your responses and then create a plan to either make peace with or celebrate your high school highlight reel!

Question	Response	Action Plan (How can I celebrate/memorialize this in my final high school days?)
Which friends am I closest to?		
Who was my toughest teacher?		
What was my least favorite class? Why?		
Who are my favorite teachers/staff members?		
What is my favorite subject?		
What are my favorite school activities?		
What do I love to do with my friends on the weekends?		
What is my favorite hangout spot in school?		
What was my all-time favorite moment in high school?		
What was my least favorite moment in high school?		

2.1: The Five Stages of Grief— High School Version

It is okay to view the changes in your friendships as losses. Have you ever heard of the five stages of grief? High school students go through something similar to that. It might not necessarily flow in order, but before senior year is over, we guarantee that you will go through a similar process:

1. Denial — This is when you realize that high school does not last forever, and life as you knew it for the past four years is coming to an end. *Where did the time go??? It can't really be over, can it?* You know those friends that you were going to have for the rest of your life? Gone. You thought that there would be more time, but before you know it, prom time is here, signaling the beginning of the end of high school life as you know it.

2. Anger — Suddenly you feel upset about the prospect of leaving high school, and maybe, just maybe, you take it out on your friends, parents, and teachers. This may also be the time when you decide that doing schoolwork is not high on your priority list because, after all, you got into college so who cares, right? This coincidentally may be the time when your school counselor calls you in for a little "pep talk."

3. Bargaining — Your anger starts to fade, and you try to figure out how to salvage your grades and create ways that your friendships will last past graduation. You may also try to *Facebook friend* your teachers, but try not to feel disappointed when they tell you that a visit around the holidays is enough.

4. Depression — This one is tricky. As a senior, you may experience feelings of sadness throughout the year as you pass milestone high school events, such as homecoming, winter formal, and prom. You might think about the past teachers you've had, the friends you met in other classes, and past boyfriends and girlfriends, and imagine having one last moment with them. It's okay to feel sad if or when this happens. Sometimes the best memories have this effect on us.

5. Acceptance — This stage will ultimately affect every high school graduate, possibly at different times. Whether it is during your last varsity game or as you walk down the graduation aisle to receive your diploma, you will know when it happens. That moment when you are content with your high school career and you realize that the next adventure is around the corner, and you are ready for it!

Grief and the sense of loss is normal, natural, and need not be disruptive to moving forward. Your Turn 2.2 invites you to consider the stages of grief, your own experience, and ways you can navigate through them. If you are able to traverse all of the stages of high school grief with as much courage and dignity as you can muster, your transition to college will be that much easier!

YOUR TURN 2.2

Exploring the Five Stages

Directions: The following questions deal with the five stages of grief and how they could potentially affect your senior year. Use these questions to develop your own prevention plan to navigate these feelings.

Area	Question	Prevention Plan (What can I do?)
Denial	1. How can I make the most out of senior year?	
	2. What are the major senior year events that I want to attend?	
Anger	1. Am I being nice to my parents? My siblings?	

Area	Question	Prevention Plan (What can I do?)
	2. Am I treating all of my friends with respect? My teachers?	
Bargaining	1. How are my grades currently? Am I doing my personal best?	
	2. Do I have the contact information for my closest friends? My favorite teachers?	
Depression	1. Am I getting enough sleep? Am I eating well?	
	2. Am I taking pictures of me and my friends at events?	
	3. Am I trying to enjoy the moment?	
Acceptance	1. Did I get a yearbook? Did my friends sign it?	
	2. Did I say goodbye to everyone that I wanted to?	
	3. What are the rules for visiting my high school as an alumnus?	

2.2: The Take Away

We hope that you take the following away from this chapter:

- Your time in high school is limited—make the best of it!
- It is natural to undergo many different emotions during senior year.
- Make plans to attend school events that you feel will bring you happy memories.
- Make a list of faculty/staff that you would like to thank/visit before you graduate.
- Get the contact information for anyone that you would like to see after high school.
- Friends are made in many different situations, and new ones will come to us at different stages all throughout our lives!

BASIC LIVING SKILLS

Every winter and spring break, former high school students, like Canadian geese migrating back their habitat after winter, return to our high school to visit their favorite teachers and friends left behind. They frequently discuss how well (or not so well) their first year in college is going and how successfully (or unsuccessfully) they made the adjustment to collegiate life. Time and time again students tell us that it was not only the academics that were daunting, but the *little things* that they had to do on their own to care for themselves that also created stress. Learning new life skills on top of environmental changes *and* a college-level course load can be overwhelming for any first-year student. It isn't difficult to learn the skills—it's just that so many other life changes are happening that it is hard for a student to feel in control. This chapter will help identify some of those areas and what skills need to be developed so that the excess energy previously consumed by stressing out can be spent studying!

We feel that the following three areas are of the most concern for students, particularly during their first year of college: *caring for oneself, laundry/cleaning, and nutrition.* The following paragraphs will describe each of these three areas in detail.

3.1: Caring for Yourself

It may sound a little childish at first, but self-care is typically the first area where people suffer most when they are feeling stressed and overwhelmed. And parents, this could be the first sign your student is dealing with a mental health or drug and alcohol issue. But it is also the area that can give you a sense of comfort and reassurance. Planning and preparing to have what you need when you need it makes all the difference in the world. When students describe how they struggled emotionally during their first month at college, they reported they were able to pull themselves out of that state by using things comforting to get them over the hump. For example, one student talked about how hard it was for him to adjust to college. He decided to keep a journal of all the new things he had learned and what he had experienced. He also made a list of questions that still needed to be answered so that when he went to visit friends and family he could share parts of his journal with them and ask for their advice. By focusing on several aspects of college life, this student was able to focus on *the now* while preparing to handle the future. This mindfulness technique is one way for students to process their experiences while learning and growing from them. This helps to reduce the worrying and "what if" thoughts that can create more stress. Mindfulness forces the student to live in the moment and move forward, rather than stressing out and focusing on negative experiences. Having cherished items close by in college that reduce pain or discomfort can make a world of difference.

YOUR TURN 3.1

Name a favorite personal item that brings you comfort and joy.	Why does it bring you comfort/joy?	Is this item something that you can bring to college with you? Why or why not?

3.2: Laundry and Cleaning

Has your student ever done their own laundry? If not, now is a great time for them to learn how to use the washer and dryer! Have them take responsibility for doing their own laundry senior year. Give instructions at the start, and gradually let them take over their own laundry care. Teach them the best way to treat clothes to avoid wrinkles and to avoid turning their undershirts and socks from white to pink. Also, not too many college students know how to iron. Helping them to master this little skill will make them the envy of their friends!

Does your student clean their own room and/or bathroom? We mean *really* clean! Most dorm rooms are small and get cluttered very quickly. If your student is a messy person, it may become a source of contention with their roommate(s). To avoid this issue, spend time creating a cleaning list with your student and develop a schedule with them to create consistency. By incorporating new cleaning habits, you may save your student years of roommate conflicts in the future.

3.3: Nutritional Needs

We all know how important eating well is for our physical and emotional health. This habit gets challenged many times during the first year of college. I'm sure you heard the term "freshman 20." This is a very real phenomenon, believe us! In college, students (especially if they have meal plan) have unlimited access to extremely large amounts of unhealthy foods and drinks, all of which they can eat in mass quantities at all hours of the day. If they are prone to stress-eating, this magnifies the situation, which can certainly lead to a negative impact on self-esteem, energy, and physical wellness, not to mention the biological hit it takes on your student's immune system. In addition, they will be exposed to large numbers of college students at very close quarters, and with a compromised immune system, they will become susceptible to any virus that comes along. It is important to spend time with your student during the senior year to help them prepare and understand the impact food has on their self-care.

VOICES FROM CAMPUS 3.1

Kelly

Kelly is a freshman at a Pennsylvania university. She was excited to get her college career going and to meet new people. Kelly found her first couple of weeks at the university very tiring. There was so much to learn and familiarize herself with that meeting basic needs was not a top priority. Kelly began to miss meals and started to grab quick, non-nutritious snacks on the go between classes. At her school, there was no shortage of junk food. Pizza was served in her dorm and in the student building all the time. Kelly began to feel worn down and tired. She thought she was getting enough sleep, but found herself waking up on and off throughout the night. Kelly eventually ended up getting every cold or flu that went through the dorm during the fall semester. The college health center provided her with medicine and advised her to get back on a health routine. She really tried hard not to miss class, but there were times that Kelly felt feverish and achy and could not get out of bed. Kelly realized missing classes in college is very different than being absent in high school. As a college student, Kelly found out very quickly that she was expected to contact her professor or classmates to get missed assignments and notes. Kelly continued to fall further and further behind in her schoolwork. Eventually, Kelly, feeling defeated, called home in frustration and tears. She was exhausted and needed some direction. Kelly's mom and dad felt strongly that she needed to see a doctor and an academic advisor to get the additional support and guidance.

3.4: Parent/Student Activity

How much responsibility does your student have in food preparation and planning in your home? Do they understand the need to balance out meals for nutritional and caloric content?

Directions: Sit down and have your student plan their menus for one week, then review it together. Does it meet the basic nutritional guidelines? What kind of nutritional needs do they have right now? Are they allergic or sensitive to particular foods? Kids are not always aware of what ingredients foods contain or which ones may give them an allergic reaction. Starting slowly, have your student plan and prepare their breakfasts for a week. It might be an interesting addition to this activity if you could get them to weigh themselves before and after the period is over for further review. Your student will need to figure out how healthy their choices are and where to get the ingredients for those meals. Will those meals give them the energy they need to get through the day? Check on their progress periodically. Were they able to follow a healthy menu? What were the challenges that still need investigating? The *next* step would be to have them plan both breakfast and lunch for the next *month*. Parents: Try to reduce your input on the decisions being made. After a month is over, have them weigh themselves again. Together, discuss the results.

Student/parent activity: during one of your parent/student outings, ask the following questions to identify what things you need to accomplish before you leave for college. As you enter the "medical" and "products" sections of the activity, create a list of "must haves" to bring with you. These are great items to ask for as graduation gifts from your extended family if they want to help. This could also alleviate some of the costs of your first year of college.

YOUR TURN 3.2

Area of Need	Question	Parent Response	Student Response
Sleep	How much sleep do you require?		
	What happens when you don't get enough sleep?		
	Do you have any needs for sleeping? Example: You may need the room to be really quiet or really dark.		
	Is there anything you can bring with you to support your needs (sleep mask, night light, etc.)?		

Area of Need	Question	Parent Response	Student Response
Medical	Do you have any medical needs? Special medicines?		
	Do you have frequent headaches? Stomachaches? Are there products that work better for you?		
	Do you require regular visits with medical specialists?		
	Do you have allergies or asthma?		
	Do you run or participate in other sports? Are there any medical needs with these activities (braces, bandages, ice packs, heating pads)?		
Products	Do you require special soaps, shampoo, or lotions?		
	Are there special go-to comfort foods?		
	Do you need a special laundry detergent?		
	Do you need razors/ shaving cream?		
	What hair products do you need (shampoo/ conditioner, spray/gel, hair clips, ties, combs, brushes, etc.)?		

(Continued)

Area of Need	Question	Parent Response	Student Response
	How will you carry these products with you to the shower room?		
	How will you keep these items organized?		
Academic Needs	Do you like certain pens, highlighters, notebooks?		
	How do you organize yourself? What are those needs?		
	What are your technology needs? How will you carry your books and other stuff?		
	How will you keep these items organized?		

3.5: The Take Away

We hope that you take the following away from this chapter:

- It is natural to undergo many different emotions during senior year. Pay attention to what your mind and body are telling you.
- Be mindful of your eating habits, and make exercise a regular part of your routine.
- Create a cleaning/laundry schedule to keep you *and* your roommate happy!
- A list of "must haves" will ensure you have all of your necessities at college to increase your level of comfort.

FINANCES AND MANAGING MONEY

Before you start this chapter, the authors would like to make it clear to the readers that we are *school counselors*, not financial planners. With that out of the way, we do have some knowledge in how to prepare students for the financial demands of college life. In this chapter, we will endeavor to impart this knowledge to students and parents alike in hopes that you enter your college experiences forewarned about the costs associated with it.

First and foremost, we cannot stress enough the importance of giving yourselves the most time possible to prepare financially for college. There are many resources available for parents to start planning for their student's college future even before they take their first steps. The state's higher education assistance website is a good place to start. The Pennsylvania Higher Education Assistance Agency's (PHEAA) website, www.pheaa.org, has excellent information regarding careers, loans, grants, scholarships, and where to find more information about them. They also direct you to the Free Application for Federal Student Aid (FAFSA), the online application every student must complete with their parents or guardians before they are considered for financial aid. Also included on the PHEAA website is the state's 529 savings plan information, which is a national savings plan that allows you as parents (and other family members) to make tax-deductible contributions to a savings account for your student up until it is time for them to attend college. What is great about the 529 plan is that grandparents, aunts, uncles, and really anyone that wants to contribute can do so in the student's name.

We know that this may sound easy, but when you consider other variables that life throws at you, planning for college may be the last thing on your mind. Realistically, parents should treat saving for college like a monthly expense, along with the rent/mortgage, food, phone, cable, and other mandatory utilities that parents must pay. Creating a budget that enables you to view your financial responsibilities takes the guesswork out of the planning process. For this daunting task, we recommend that parents contact their local banking institution, many of which offer sound college planning advice (along with personal loans for college), or financial planner. The most important takeaway is to do something, *anything*, to prepare for college and create a plan that works for you.

For the seniors reading this book—fear not, we haven't forgotten about you! Your role in this process is just as vital. Whether you have seen your parents budgeting and planning for your future or not, it is important that you create a college budget as well. By now, you may or may not have part-time employment. Did you save anything from your job or jobs? Hopefully the answer is yes! If not, now is the time to start!

If you don't have one already, ask your parents to help you set up a bank account, preferably one that that is both local to you and your future college/university; that both you and your parents share; and that has good interest rates for credit cards, personal loans for students for college, and low-to-no fees for withdrawing money from ATMs. Shopping around for the right bank will save you a lot of money in the long run! Our suggestion is to find a *credit union*—a member-owned non-profit banking institution that usually has competitive rates compared to the banks that are solely for profit.

Along with finding the right bank for you, it is important to learn about credit cards and their benefits and pitfalls before you leave for college. There are many tempting offers credit card companies will make to you once you are on campus. Our advice is to learn as much about credit cards as possible before you make decisions on whether to get one. Additionally, ask your parents what they know about credit cards and consult them before you apply for one! If you don't have the finances to pay regularly for them, they could have long-lasting, *negative* effects on your *credit report*—a document that follows you forever and is based on your ability to pay for things on time. Your credit report affects your ability to purchase a car, house, or even a cell phone!

You will also need to have a grown-up conversation with your parents about how much money they (or other family members) have saved on your behalf. You may find out that someone in your family owned stock in Apple and left you a million dollars! Or maybe not. But at the very least, you will know how much (or how little) you have saved for college, and that information is better than no information! Once this is figured out, you can work with your parents on how to finance college. A word of advice: No matter whether you think you will qualify for financial aid or not, always fill out the Free Application for Federal Student Aid (FAFSA). If this form is not filled out, you are automatically disqualifying yourself from federal or state loans and grants, as well as the many scholarships that can be offered to you through your college.

Speaking of scholarships, as a senior, it is your responsibility to start looking for as many scholarships as possible to help pay for college. While there are many scholarships out there for ninth graders through eleventh graders, the majority of the available scholarships are for seniors. Do not wait to get accepted into a college to start looking for scholarships. We have seen many scholarships go unnoticed in the fall of senior year because students were applying to colleges and waiting to hear back from their schools first before looking for scholarships. Typically, scholarships have specific requirements that they are looking for in a student. While there are the more traditional scholarships for students with high academic and athletic abilities, there are also scholarships given for reasons that you might not have ever considered! For example, there are scholarships for very tall people, very short people, twins, left-handed students, Boy and Girl Scouts, students from underrepresented groups, and students that grew up on farms. Also, if you were involved in extracurricular activities in high school, like the Rotary Club, Association for Marketing Students (DECA), or the Exchange Club of America, your local chapter may have a scholarship for you. Students applying to specific majors will have scholarships earmarked specifically for them as well. And there may be local families, clubs, and charities that give money to deserving seniors every year in your community that you never even heard of. How do you find out about these scholarships? You see your *school counselor*, of course! If they do not have this information available, We are positive they can direct you to the right place or person. Voices From Campus 4.1 relates the experience of one student who took advantage of a unique scholarship opportunity.

VOICES FROM CAMPUS 4.1

Jack

I remember going to see my counselor in September of my senior year about scholarships. He reminded me that our counseling office organizes scholarships every month for seniors to review! He also told me about a program called Naviance (we use it every year, but I always forget about it!) and a national database of scholarships to look through. It seemed like a lot of work! But once I started using it, things really came together. I got a list of scholarships to apply to, and I ended up getting a few thousand dollars for college! One was because I saw a scholarship posting for a scholarship for agriculture majors, which is my future major. It took me twenty minutes to fill out, and I won $1,000. This is money that I wouldn't have had if I didn't ask and research the scholarships in my counselor's office.

Staying organized is very important if you are looking for scholarships. As we mentioned before, scholarships are given for many reasons; the trick is to make sure that you meet the criteria so you don't waste very important time applying for scholarships for which you don't qualify. On the following page is a worksheet we created to help you stay organized in your quest for scholarships. It will also help you keep track of the various things they are looking for in an applicant.

Figure 4.1 Scholarship Worksheet

Scholarship Name			
Scholarship Amount			
Deadline			
Unique Criteria			
Essay Required?			
Transcript Required? • *Official or unofficial?*			
GPA Requirement? • If yes, what is it? • Weighted or unweighted?			
Email or snail mail?			
Address?			
Additional Information:			

As the financial part of your preparation for college starts to work itself out, your attention can now turn toward budgeting practices for next year. Some of the things that your parents provide for you now will become your responsibility. Specifically, it will become your responsibility to use your money wisely, otherwise you may not have money on hand to buy or do the things that you really want to do or need. For example, it may not be prudent to buy those shoes that you saw online if you don't have money for toothpaste and soap the following week! As you begin to think about using your money smartly, think about the following terms.

Income: Income is money you receive that you will use to purchase the items you need. This could come on a weekly, biweekly, monthly, or semester schedule. Sources of income may include your parents, campus employment, scholarships, loans, etc.

Fixed Expenses: Fixed expenses are not negotiable, and they generally do not change in amount. Examples are rent, car insurance, and cell phone bills.

Flexible Expenses: Expenses are flexible when they vary in amount from month to month, or semester to semester. Examples include entertainment, gas for your car, eating out, and buying clothing.

There are many examples of college budgets available online. We believe that creating a semester budget would be an appropriate place to begin. If you feel like a monthly or even yearly budget is more appropriate for you, then we recommend that you do what is best for your needs.

Student/parent activity: The following is an example of a semester budget. With your parents, list dollar amounts for each income/expense item that is relevant to you. If there are some items that are not included on the sheet, please add them in the space provided.

Figure 4.2 College Budget Worksheet

Income	Semester
From Jobs (after taxes)	
From Parents/Family Members Financial Aid	
Scholarships	
Other_____	
Other_____	
Other_____	
Total Income:	
Fixed Expenses:	
Cell Phone	
Car Insurance	
Food/Meal Plan	
Tuition	
Loan Payments	
Credit Card Payments	
Utilities (Cable/Electric)	
Other_____	
Other_____	
Other_____	
Total Fixed Expenses:	
Flexible Expenses:	
Books	
Clothing	
Entertainment (movies, concerts)	
Groceries	
Gas	
Other_____	
Other_____	
Other_____	
Total Flexible Expenses:	
Total Income:	
Total Expenses (Fixed + Flexible):	
Amount Left Over (Income − Expenses):	

Creating a budget takes time and commitment. You will not be able to accurately determine every aspect of your financial needs through your first year of college; however, the more you plan for what lies ahead, the less stress you (and your parents) will experience. Continue to discuss budgeting with your parents or your school counselor. Also keep in mind that your future college's financial aid representative will have tips to help you save, plan, and budget your way to a successful first year of college. Note: If you're looking for more information about planning financially for college, *A Student's Guide to Financial Issues/ Money Matters*, which is part of this series, will explore this topic on a deeper level. You may find this to be an excellent resource on the issue of managing finances and making financial decisions as they relate to funding a college (and post-college) education.

VOICES FROM CAMPUS 4.2

Massiah

In my first semester of college, I was so excited to be there that I didn't watch how much money I was spending. Instead of using my meal plan, I would hang out in the evening, miss dinner time, and then order take-out with my friends late at night. By October, I was out of money in my flex account, and I had no spare cash to get snacks. I worked in a pizza shop during my senior year and had some money saved, but my bank account was dropping—fast! My parents told me that I needed to spend my money better and that they weren't going to send me money every time I asked. I decided to get a part-time job on campus in the ice cream shop. Now I have extra money on the side to buy the things I want without begging my parents every time. Since my paycheck isn't that big, I need to watch my spending if I want to make it last. It helps now that I've made a budget for myself to see where my money is going. My money situation was so much better in the second semester than the first!

4.3: The Take Away

We hope that you take the following away from this chapter:

- It is never too early to save and plan financially for college.
- Apply for financial aid, even if you and your parents think that you won't qualify.
- Find a bank or credit union that best meets you needs and is convenient for you to access.
- Consult your parents, or financial experts before applying for credit cards.
- Apply for scholarships all throughout your senior year. Ask your school counselor for assistance!
- Creating a college budget will help to ensure that you have money when you need it.

EXPOSING YOURSELF TO OTHER CULTURES

At this point in the book, you have (hopefully) read Chapter 2 and now understand the importance of making new friends in college. As you are doing this, it is very likely that the new friends you meet will come from someplace different than you, with cultures, values, and beliefs that may or may not be like your own. Because of this, it is important that you approach potential new friends with an open mind, a sense of respect, and a desire to meet people whose journey to college may or may not reflect yours.

5.1: Diversity in Many Forms

Diversity comes in all forms that are not always obvious. Let's take Lois and Clark for example. Clark, a freshman at Metropolis University, is in a Sociology 101 class with Lois, and they are part of the same break-out group in class.

While they didn't know each other prior to meeting on campus, their placement in Sociology 101 provided them with a shared common experience and the grounds upon which to get to know each other. As was true for all the members of their sociology group, Clark and Lois could connect around common experiences such as the sociology class, their professor, respective majors, homecoming plans, where they live on campus, the lunch room, the library, the food in the cafeteria, and of course group projects. These were all fertile topics for conversation and opportunities to deepen their connection. But even with a shared experience, with time and personal disclosure, both Lois and Clark will come to understand the ways in which they are different, and how their diversity could actually enrich both of their experiences and strengthen their connections.

5.2: Culture and Its Effects

When we think of the word "culture," we often think of far-off lands and people with unique language, dress, and styles. Such an image is one that clearly highlights culture, but cultural differences occur in our own background. The website *LiveScience* (Zimmerman, 2018) describes *culture* as "the characteristics and knowledge of a particular group of people, encompassing language, religion, cuisine, social habits, music and arts," so we may find—as Lois and Clark did—cultural diversity right in our own group.

Consider the 'culture' experienced by both Lois and Clark as revealed by the daily routine they followed prior to entering college. Clark, for example, grew up on a farm in a rural area. He began his mornings by assisting his parents with managing the crops and livestock. The day started quite early for Clark, completing his chores, then eating a large country breakfast followed by walking 1.5 miles to school. Lois, on the other hand, grew up in a city 50 miles from Clark. Her morning routine while in high school involved connecting online with her best friend, arranging for a meeting place, and enjoying a latte as they both rode the train to the connecting bus that took them to their private high school on the other side of Metropolis. Lois and Clark, to most people, look similar—both share the same ethnicity and dress in a comparable fashion. If one were to go on appearances alone, they might believe that they share many things in common. However, their cultural experiences are entirely different from each other. Can you imagine the differences in their morning routine, or the music they listened to while preparing for school, or even the interests and values they learned are the result of growing up in their own unique cultures?

We don't need to think about foreign lands to see the existence of culture. It is important to realize that no matter where and how one grows up, everyone possesses a culture that is unique to them. That uniqueness should be honored and valued. Our culture is part of the multitude of experiences that make us who we are and, as such, is worth understanding. Your Turn 5.1 invites you to recall and list experiences that may be unique to you and your family.

YOUR TURN 5.1

Reflecting on Culture

With your parents' assistance (maybe even your grandparents!), sit down together and identify important cultural traits and traditions that your family holds and/or practices regularly.

What ethnicity (or ethnicities) does your family identify with? What about your parents and grandparents?

Does your family practice organized religion? What are some of the major beliefs/ values that you have learned?

What favorite foods does your family enjoy? Are there specific foods/desserts that you feel are unique to your family?

What major holidays are celebrated by your family? Does your family do anything different on this day than your friends? Which holidays are the most special to *you*?	
What traditions are celebrated in your family, and how?	
What activities does your family like to do together?	

5.3: Self-Enrichment: Engaging with Diversity

As we leave Lois and Clark in sociology class, let's discuss the many opportunities *outside* of class to meet someone from a different culture. This opportunity to expand your awareness and appreciation for other cultures should not be ignored. It is, or can be, truly enriching.

College residence halls typically hold many social events where you can meet people from different floors (or the other side of your hallway) and learn about similarities, differences, as well as common interests. While it may feel awkward initiating the first step, remember you all have one big conversation starter in common—you live in the same building! In addition to formal or informal gatherings at your residence hall, most campuses hold various fairs, which are wonderful places to learn about different groups and the causes and experiences that bind them together. For example, Lois, whom we mentioned previously, attended a career fair on campus. As she walked about the fair she came upon a table that was sharing information on animal husbandry as a major and providing applications for the Future Farmers of America Club. As she was paging through the information, being clueless about both animal husbandry and future farmers, she remembered that Clark told her about his high school version of the club and that he was its president. Lois was intrigued about the rural lifestyle and how different it was from the way she was raised. She spoke with Clark about the club and, with his encouragement, signed up to attend an upcoming meeting. Given her background, Lois knew she was about to encounter individuals with experiences different than her own, with numerous perspectives that would enrich and expand her understanding of others.

5.4: Moving from Our Comfort Zone

For most of us, entering college, with its many opportunities and challenges, can be stressful and anxiety-provoking. Under these conditions it is not unusual to feel as if our world has been shaken to its core and that we are in need of a safe place. This desire for safety and familiarity may lead us to connect with people from our neighborhood or our high school. Yes, meeting others from different backgrounds and cultures can be a bit nerve-wracking. But it is a cost worth paying for the personal enrichment you will receive.

When reaching out for new connections, it helps to find an activity or a place that is structured and safe. Most of the clubs and activities provided on campus can serve as *safe spaces* for their members. *Merriam-Webster* (2018) describes a safe space as any place intended to be free of bias, conflict, criticism, or potentially threatening actions, ideas, or conversations. When engaging with others, it is important first observe. Remember that you are a *visitor* in their group, and it is imperative that you are respectful of the experiences of the attendees. The values that you hold should not be imposed upon others in the group.

Experiencing people, activities, and cultures that are outside of our comfort zone can be a little unnerving, but also exciting. As such, we invite you to consider Your Turn 5.2.

YOUR TURN 5.2

Venturing Out

Directions: If you have not yet entered campus, you may want to consider attending, along with your parents, an event that is culturally different than your own. Connect with a friend and try something outside of your own world of experience. Look through your local newspaper or on-campus posters and find local music/food festivals, parades, art exhibits, theater performances, or other similar events. You can even check churches in the area for both their worship services and socials.

After the experience, complete the following activity. With your parents (if they accompanied you) or friends discuss the following. Be sure to consider what was the same and what was different from your family's culture.

Name of the event/location			
What was the most exciting part about attending the event?			
What was the least interesting part?			
What aspects of the event were different from the culture in which you grew up?			
What practices/ traditions were similar to your culture?			

Are there any
similar events or
groups at your
future college?

5.5: Making Initial Connections

We know that you possess fundamental social skills and know the basics about how to engage with others. But believe it or not, sometimes the obvious is forgotten. As you begin to interact with others from a different culture, remember a few simple guidelines.

- Keep it simple: Make your introduction simple and to the point. Start with "Hi, I'm _____" or "My name is _____," and let things expand naturally from there.

- Start with that which is common: This is where your common interests will come in handy (same school, class, club, etc.). Avoid questions that are personal in nature in first meetings—family (particularly where someone is from), religion, and politics are all potentially off-putting topics if someone does not share the same views as you.

- Focus on the here and now: Staying focused on the event at hand, or something neutral like the weather, movies, television, or the latest popular culture news, is a terrific way to get to know someone without upsetting or offending them.

- Listen: Listen for understanding. There may be words or phrases or references that are unfamiliar to you. Repeat that word or phrase (to indicate that you heard), but then share that it is a new term or idea and explain that you would love to hear more about it. It is in listening and reflecting on what you are hearing that you will begin to move deeper into the relationship and understanding the other person's perspective.

5.6: Risky, Yet Worth It

Making new friends always involves some level of risk. You are putting yourself out there emotionally, and there is the chance that you could be rejected by the other person. While this may be true, ask yourself this question: what if the next person I meet forever changes my life? Meeting new people is a way to enhance your knowledge of the people around you. It is also an opportunity for others to get to know you as a person, along with the unique gifts that you offer the world. This was certainly true for Ken (see Voices From Campus 5.1).

VOICES FROM CAMPUS 5.1

Ken

I remember meeting Ken freshman year. At first, I didn't think that we had anything in common! I was a skinny track kid, and he was a football player from the middle of nowhere who looked like he could lift a small car. Every time I returned to our dorm room after class, he was doing push-ups and listening to music I thought was really weird. I never heard it on the radio stations I listened to, and I assumed it was a country thing. Boy, was I wrong! One day, I just flat-out asked him what he was playing, and he said that it was the Beatles. The Beatles? You mean the group with the guy who once sang a song with Michael Jackson? Ken proceeded to educate me on the Beatles and every album in his collection. I also shared my music with him. From there, we started talking about where and how we grew up, and we found out that we were a lot alike after all! One day, I entered our room and there was Ken, still doing push-ups, but listening to music from *my* collection! Through music, we formed a friendship that lasted beyond freshman year.

5.7: The Take Away

We hope that you take the following away from this chapter:

- Diversity comes in many forms. Be open to the idea of learning about races and cultures that are different than your own.
- Research your family traditions by talking with your parents, grandparents, aunts, uncles, and cousins about your family history and culture.
- Attend activities that promote and support the diversity that exists in your college.

5.8: References

LiveScience. What is culture? Retrieved from https://www.livescience.com/21478-what-is-culture-definition-of-culture.html

SELF-ADVOCACY

As much as we would like to believe that each one of our high school graduates goes off to college and has a wonderful experience, we have learned that this is not always the case. The students that leave college and come back to speak with us share what led them to withdraw from what they thought was their "dream." We learned that the main reason most students "give up" during their first year is due to their lack of self-advocacy skills. When a student enters college, there is an expectation that they are now adults and have all of the necessary skills to make adult decisions. Students do feel an increased sense of independence, which means they *want* to do everything on their own without any help or support, but don't always know how. Some of our students reported not feeling comfortable with asking directions, making phone calls, or even setting up billing for utilities. Additionally, we see an impaired ability to identify a problem and solve it with the appropriate person. Colleges provide loads of resources for their students, but the ability to identify needs and have the self-advocacy skills to ask how and where they can get support or direction is what is needed. College is not like high school, where teachers will come to you when they notice something is wrong. The ball is now in their hands, and they have to run with it! In this chapter, we will review levels of self-advocacy of students and learn ways to improve those skills.

Students require self-advocacy skills for a successful transition from high school to any post-secondary institution. The process should begin in the early high school years (even earlier, if possible). In addition to self-advocacy skills, it is important for students who struggle with mental health or intellectual disabilities to be aware of their rights and how to get their message across assertively. Below is a quiz that parents and students can take to check how strong of an advocate they are. This quiz can then be used to determine what you both can work on in the next year to strengthen their skills.

YOUR TURN 6.1

Self-Advocacy Quiz

True or False?	Student	Parent
I am aware of my interests, strengths, and limitations.		
I know the difference between a want and a need.		
I can solve problems on my own or with others.		
I know how to set goals and reach them.		
I am able to talk about problems I have with others.		
I know my rights as a student.		
I take responsibility for things when I am wrong.		
I am a good listener.		
I have the ability to compromise.		
It is easy for me to make decisions.		
I have strong assertiveness skills.		

After completing the exercise, spend some time reviewing the answers that differ. Why are your answers different? What examples can you give one another to support your answers? If you both have the same false answers, then perhaps this is an area that you need to work on before heading off to college.

6.1: Understanding Yourself

A large part of self-advocacy is learning how to truly know yourself. Understanding yourself means you know your personal preferences and how they differ from those around you. Being comfortable with, or at least tolerant of, those who have different personalities, interests, and preferences than you is an important part of growing and evolving as a human being. That level of comfort starts by first exploring your personal background and feelings. What makes you tick, and what ticks you off? Knowing your interests and likes can provide you with a social connection almost immediately upon entering college. The first few weeks away from home can be a lonely time for some students. Going to a club meeting or an activity of interest will help you to find other students with similar networks. Check to see if your school has an activity fair during the opening weeks of the semester, and go to it! Doing something that you love and enjoy will help reduce loneliness and increase your sense of belonging to your college. Having that feeling of belonging is important, especially in the first year. Students frequently say they leave college because they felt they did not belong—that *it just didn't feel right.* In most cases, those students did not take the initiative to seek out interests and meet people they were comfortable being around at college. Most colleges are much larger than high schools, so it can take a good bit of personal initiative to find other people who you can enjoy being with during your free time. It is also just as important to try some activities that you are not familiar with in order to broaden your horizons. Most colleges attract students from all walks of life, and what better way to learn about differences than in a college setting. Putting yourself out there to try something new could be a great way to meet people different than yourself. You may develop passions and interests that you may not have had the opportunity to experience in your high school or local community.

6.2: How to Solve Problems

Problem-solving is a systematic process that we use every day. Some of us are better at it than others. Students are just beginning to form their own strategies to resolve conflicts with their peers. Independence—that is, being on your own and making your own decisions—can be a struggle for some students, especially ones who did not have to make many decisions independent of their parents during their high school years. Many of their decisions during the first couple of years of college could be life changing, more so than any previous time. The more you practice the art of problem-solving the better you will get at the task. Understanding the steps and applying them in the last couple of years of high school will reduce stress and frustration later in college. Next are some steps that may appear simple, but you might be surprised as to how many high school students do not use them.

Step one: Identifying the true problem. Is the problem a person, situation, or a feeling? Is it something else? It is important to accurately locate the source first or this step will have to be revisited. Most of the time, this needs to be done alone, unless you have someone very close to you that understands the whole situation. Step two: Brainstorm solutions. Looking at a problem from all different angles, not only from your perspective, is very important in this step. Write everything down to review later with a fresh perspective. Sometimes it is useful to ask others to brainstorm ideas as well. Look at each of the ideas and determine if one is a viable solution. Finally, step three: Ask yourself "Will this really work in my situation?" Focus on those solutions that answer this question first.

As with many things in life, problem-solving is often aided by engaging another person who brings an alternative perspective and a different skill set. The following activity invites both the student and parent to practice the problem-solving steps listed above.

PARENT/STUDENT ACTIVITY 6.1

Many issues or problems can arise with students in senior year, when the time comes to choose the right college, prom date, or where they are going for senior week. During senior year, identify a problem and then try the steps above. Parent: Walk the student through the process first, then gradually allow them to implement the steps. The more your student can introduce these steps into their daily lives the more it will help them when they are stressed or overwhelmed. This modeling process can not only be used for college, but also for many years to follow. The more students practice these skills in college, the better they will be at handling life's increasing challenges once their college years are over.

6.3: Listening Skills

Listening skills are the foundation of all self-advocacy. Being able to listen effectively and be heard is an art that is not as simple as it sounds. It is not only the words people are saying but the emotions behind those words and the nonverbal actions that are on display. The inability to translate verbal and nonverbal cues is at the center of most miscommunications. Are you a good listener? What can you do to improve your skills? Are you always thinking about what you are going to say instead of listening to the other person?

6.4: Assertiveness Skills

Assertiveness skills are difficult to build in high school. Peer influences and the culture of high school make it hard for students to develop their individuality. Students believe there is a certain image or expectation to which they must conform. There is a lot of emphasis on looking like everyone else and having similar interests. In college, students are exposed to people from all walks of life, and the social norms they were used to in high school may drastically differ. This could be a great opportunity for a student to find others with similar interests, likes, and even quirks, that bring with them a sense of belonging not experienced before.

Assertiveness allows a student to stand up for themselves by expressing their thoughts and feelings in a direct, honest, and appropriate way. Being assertive also means, after listening and hearing the other person's thoughts and feelings, being able to admit that you have made a mistake *and* being able to apologize for that mistake. It is not easy to listen to and understand another person's views when they are different from your own. Empathy, the power of understanding another person's viewpoint, will help get your statement across without name-calling or blaming. In our experience, we have seen many high school students say "yes" to other students or adults when they really want to say "no." This passive response is usually not helpful to the student, nor the other person. Practicing saying "no" and explaining why they are saying "no" can start a student on their way towards assertiveness.

PARENT/STUDENT ACTIVITY 6.2

Parents, when a difference of opinion comes along (like whether your daughter should share a beach house with three boys for senior week or whether your student is ready to get a driver's license) and you can sense everyone is not listening or using their assertiveness skills, try this exercise. First, sit down with your student when a conflict arises. It will most likely be a bit uncomfortable at first. Start the conversation by recognizing that each person has a different opinion and may not be hearing one another. Without interruption, have each person state their opinion and give their perspective. Before the next person responds, they will need to summarize what the first person has said before sharing their position. Then repeat these steps after each thought. This can be a real challenge for some people, but it allows each party to recognize that they heard what the other person said rather than always thinking about what they are going to say next. Another activity would be to replace the word "you" with "I feel" when expressing your opinion. An example of this would be a parent stating "I feel uncomfortable with you staying in the same house with three boys because…" instead of "You can't stay for a week in the same house with three boys!" These steps improve listening skills and allow for the other person to better understand the thoughts and feelings behind the conflicting opinions. It makes communication clearer and less likely to end in a defensive battle. This process builds self-worth, self-reliance, and assertiveness—all traits valuable to a student's success in college.

VOICES FROM CAMPUS 6.1

Rick

Rick just made it through his first year of college. He was a strong student in high school and had lots of friends, but he found it difficult to locate other people with the same interests as himself. He worked hard at getting his schoolwork done but felt it was too much of a challenge. Rick seemed to not "get" what the professors wanted from him, and in turn he needed to redo many things or accept a bad grade. Time management was something Rick never struggled with before, but he found it to be an issue now. Rick almost decided not to go back to his school after winter break until his resident advisor (RA) sat with him to check on his progress. Rick's RA talked to him about all of the academic resources available. Rick remembered hearing about this and other resources during new student orientation in the summer, but at the time he did not think that he would need them. The biggest concern Rick's professors had was with the quality of his writing. Rick's RA told him the university had a writing center. All he needed to do was bring the assignment to them, and they would help him correct it so he could then hand in the assignment. It was a great resource that the RA used all the time, and he let Rick know that it was available to all students. He also told Rick that it was important to reach out to others if things aren't going well and that he was lucky the RA noticed he was distressed. Rick was surprised that his RA used the writing center, and he did not seem embarrassed about receiving help. Rick decided to go back to school the next semester. When he returned from winter break, Rick was going to investigate the writing center. He also wanted to look into other resources that the college has to support him not only with his academics but with his social life as well.

6.6: The Take Away

We hope that you take the following away from this chapter:

- Self-advocacy is an essential skill to master in order to get your academic, social, and emotional needs met in college.
- Strong communication, listening, and assertiveness skills will improve your ability to self-advocate.
- Self-advocacy is a *learned* behavior, acquired by modeling others, and lots of practice!

FACING SPECIAL NEEDS AND CHALLENGES

Many of the parents and students we meet with understand the importance of going to college, but most are worried about the emotional well-being of their student once they are there. College can be exciting, but for some it also can be stressful and overwhelming. If your student has any preexisting medical or mental health concerns, the transition can be a trigger for a decline in health. Warning: The beginning of this chapter may cause a bit of anxiety because we ask so many questions and introduce a lot of "what ifs." Later in the chapter, you will create a plan that will provide direction and help prepare you and your student for future situations. This goal of this chapter is to reduce worrisome thoughts. Whether a student has asthma or agoraphobia, it is important to create a prevention plan now for their new college home later.

Use the following questions to guide decision-making as you make strong, effective plans for your transition. We want to help you increase the parent-student bond, reduce stress, and set things up for a successful college experience.

Question 1: How Far Away from Home Is the College?

One of the most common questions we hear from parents and students about going off to college is "How far should my student go away from home when they are struggling with medical and/or mental health issues?" In this case, we recommend a compromise by considering colleges or universities that are less than two to three hours away. This provides the student with the growth of independence, but they are still close enough that you can get there quickly if needed. In other words, far enough away where you would want to contact them in advance to let them know you are coming. You would not want to drive two or three hours to find out they are not there. This gives students a sense of privacy, and it allows the student to think about the concern first before hopping in the car to drive home if things get a little difficult. A large part of college life is building decision-making skills. One way to determine an appropriate distance is to draw a circle on a map indicating the appropriate distance around your home. That will give you a location window to narrow down your student's choices for colleges and universities. This can also be done online in several college search tools. As they get closer to making a final college decision, you can assess your student's condition and use that to create your list of options.

Question 2: How Long Does It Take to Get to the College by Car?

The college may be an hour away by *plane*, but if your student needs lots of support this could become costly.

Question 3: Does the College Have Mental and Physical Health Supports in Place to Address My Individual Needs?

These questions can be answered online or during college visits. It is important to make sure that your college has the appropriate resources readily available, especially if your student does not have their own transportation. Many freshmen are not allowed to keep vehicles on campus.

Question 4: How Much of Those Supports Will Be Provided by Outside Agencies—Not Available on Campus?

Most colleges have infirmaries and counseling centers, which can assess and meet basic mental and physical health needs; however, if your student requires specialists, they will need to be researched and located.

Question 5: Can Your Student Seek Their Own Medical Interventions Independently?

If your student has a diagnosed medical or mental health condition, they may not be comfortable seeking out care if it goes beyond their ability to manage on their own. An example of this could be a diabetic student that is experiencing complications, or a student with a newly-diagnosed mental health condition. Understanding the importance of seeking additional support and the ability to create a *safety net* at college, especially when things are not going well, is an important step that students need to take to safeguard their health.

Question 6: Will Your Student Be Able to Access Help if Needed?

Some people are more comfortable with asking for help than others. College is a time to gain independence and experience life, but there may come a time when your student needs to reach out for help. For some this may take consistent practice. How social is your student? Is it easy or hard for them to make friends and find support?

Socialization can be a struggle for many people, and living in a college environment with thousands of people you don't know can be scary. The best way to deal with this is to encourage your student to find and join—as soon as possible—as many clubs and organizations as they are interested in. It is much easier to converse with people who have similar interests. Many college clubs and organizations have social media sites as well, so your student can research these organizations beforehand.

Question 7: Is Size of the College a Factor When Making the Decision for a Student with Medical or Mental Health Needs?

Another factor when choosing a school for students who struggle with a physical or mental health issue is the size of the college/university. Larger colleges and universities typically deal with tens of thousands of students. Students that attend these schools often tell us that they felt like a number while attending. This makes it hard to build a rapport with the faculty and staff—connections that are so vital for the retention of students. In contrast, the options available (majors, clubs, groups) at larger colleges are vast. It is in smaller colleges students find they get more individualized care and support. In smaller college settings, faculty and staff oftentimes have the flexibility to act more like mentors and guide students to appropriate options. However, there is a downside because smaller colleges also offer fewer majors, activities, and resources. These are things that you should investigate before a final college decision is made. It will be worth the time and effort to create a list of viable options to pick from before a final decision is made in the spring.

7.1: Mental Health Concerns

There are many different mental health concerns that affect young adults. Below are some common issues that students face that can affect class attendance and stress levels. We have selected several to focus on, and by completing Parent/Student Activity 7.1 at the end of this chapter, you should better be able to individualize your student's plan according to their needs.

Anxiety

Over the last several years, we have seen an increase in anxiety issues among our high school students. Going off to college certainly raises many issues of worry and fear for both students and parents. The best way to reduce these concerns is being prepared and equipped to face the issues if they surface. Students and parents need to work together to identify the major triggers of anxiety. Talk about this together. Students: how do you know you are feeling anxious? What are your symptoms? What has worked in the past when you have felt this way? Are you able to get access to those coping strategies? For example, it could be that walking next to a stream in a park close to your home helps to reduce your anxious thoughts. While it isn't realistic to come home every time you feel anxious, you may be able to find a park close by the campus that is a great replacement. Finding and locating these coping locations or strategies beforehand may prove to be beneficial, as it is difficult to locate and implement a new strategy when you are struggling.

Depression

The amount of change that happens within the first few months of leaving home for college is extraordinary. Leaving home and school can be a great loss for students. Moving to a brand-new environment can be even more challenging to a student who struggles with depression. Adapting to the college as quickly as possible is vital to creating a positive sense of well-being. It is certainly normal for your student to feel homesick in the first month or two, but if it lasts the greater part of the semester, then intervention is needed. All colleges and universities have counseling centers. We recommend that you encourage your student to find out where that center is and schedule an appointment before they even leave home. By visiting the counseling center in advance, the student can start to build a resilient relationship with the mental health workers at their future home—much needed if a relapse occurs once they are on campus.

Learning Disabilities

Students with a learning disability may find college to be a bit of struggle at first, so it is very important, like we advised for students with mental health concerns, that they find the place on campus that will give them the academic support they need. Most colleges have a specific department to support and guide students with learning concerns. The key to getting academic support is that the student must initiate a meeting with the department and discuss their needs. Bringing a copy of the Individualized Education Plan (IEP), Evaluation Report (ER) or 504 service agreement with them is very beneficial for students when they visit. Colleges really don't want to hear from parents when it comes to academic services. Most universities and colleges require an updated evaluation report, usually within three years. They want to know what your student's current academic abilities are and what recommendations were made to support them. Colleges and universities vary greatly on the type and degree of services they will provide. State-funded university systems may offer more services, as they are required by law to do so. Most colleges and universities have academic support centers in addition to learning support centers. An example of this would be a writing center. This has been helpful for many of our students. For example, nearly every student must take an English course during their freshman year. If they finish the writing assignment before the deadline, they are able submit it to the writing center for feedback. The writing center corrects the paper and returns it to the student. The student can then make changes and hand it in.

These services are available for *every* student. Locating these centers and including them in a plan of support will be important. Setting up a goal to connect with the academic and learning support centers within the first two weeks of school takes the pressure off of scrambling to find the centers when they are in academic crisis mode!

Attention Deficit Hyperactivity Disorder (ADHD)

Students who are challenged with ADHD will need to prepare for many changes once they enter college, particularly with organization, time management and the completion of their class assignments. Many of these students receive support and reminders from school staff and parents. Once they are living on their own, they will not have parents and teachers reminding them when something is due for their classes. Before entering college, students and parents should review what strategies worked and didn't in high school, and transition those approaches to time constraints they will inevitably face in college. Being able to independently function in these areas should be the focus of the senior year for the student to be successful in college.

Medical Issues and Chronic Conditions

Students and parents, it is important for you to meet with your family doctor to determine what medical attention is needed for your chronic condition if you are far away from home. Meeting with the university's health center to discuss your student's medical needs is vital. Also discuss a plan of what to do when the health center is closed. What resources does the health center provide to support your student? How close is the nearest hospital? And how good is it? What should the student do at 2:00 a.m. if they are not feeling well? What are the bottom-line symptoms that indicate the need to call 911?

Another important item to do if your student is being treated by a pediatrician is to migrate them to a family doctor that deals with adult health concerns *before* they go off to college. This will help to alleviate some confusion when they come home after their first year and are either forced to change their doctor then or, even worse, when they call to make a doctor's appointment in their new, adult-sounding voice and are asked who the child is that they are calling for!

Allergies

Allergy concerns can range from getting a stuffy nose during pollen season to having difficulty breathing due to chest congestion. Understanding the triggers for these reactions and knowing what to do when they occur will alleviate these concerns. Parents, make sure that your student knows how to deal with their allergy symptoms on their own or knows how to get help from the school health center when needed. Food allergies can even be more challenging. Some foods cause such violent allergic reactions that an EpiPen may be needed. It is mandatory that you inform the health center and those that will be closest to you on campus (roommates, resident advisor, professors) of any serious life-threatening allergy concerns so that potentially dangerous situations can be handled quickly.

7.2: Other Concerns: Suicide

We realize that it is hard to image your student ever having suicidal thoughts, but it is a potential reality for which you should be prepared. Suicide is the second leading cause of death for college-age youth (CDC WISQARS, 2015). Students go through 12 years of primary and secondary education to get into college, secure a job, and pursue happiness. College can be a real academic wake-up call for some students, and this may be the first time your student has had to face this type of struggle. Every human being is complex and may react differently when faced with challenges. Students who do not do well in the first semester can become emotionally devastated. Our students have been told by society that going to college is the only way they can "make something" of themselves. Students can find themselves in a hopeless situation when they are faced with the challenges of higher education and do not feel as if they are able to succeed. Reaching out to your student on a regular basis, just to check in, is crucial. Even if your student does not have any of the above concerns, or even if they blow you off because they have "something important to do," you need to keep reaching out to them as much as possible and as much as they allow. When you are touching base with each other, do a mental check to see if your student is exhibiting any of the following changes:

1. Physical Changes—difficulty falling or staying asleep, difficulty waking up, eating too little or too much, loss of interest in routine activities, crying spells, fatigue, unexplained physical pain.

2. Academic Changes—difficulty with focus and concentration, trouble making decisions, not completing schoolwork, in a "fog."

3. Emotional Changes—feeling worthless, hopeless, sad, isolated, alone, overwhelmed, agitated over a prolonged period, feeling life is not worth living, socially withdrawing.

These signs and symptoms can indicate your student is depressed, suicidal, overwhelmed, or lacking proper coping skills. Don't hesitate to ask for help from the college counseling center, preferably with your student's consent. That is yet another reason to have all those phone numbers and university contacts available before a problem arises. Most importantly, don't be afraid to ask your son or daughter directly if they are experiencing suicidal thoughts. You will *not* be putting this thought in their head. If you don't get a clear "No way! I would never do that," then the answer is *yes*. Even if they say just a little or maybe, consider it a "yes" and find help for them immediately.

It is important to always:

1. Express your concern about what you are observing in their behavior

2. Ask your student how they are doing or feeling

3. Listen to your student—and take everything they say seriously

4. Reassure your student that help is available

5. Contact a college staff member **immediately** if you suspect suicidal thoughts are present.

It is important to never:

1. Ignore warning signs of unusual or uncharacteristic behavior
2. Act shocked or be judgmental about what your student says
3. Negative advice not helpful to how your student is feeling
4. Provide false reassurances
5. Dismiss their problems or minimize the threats your student is making

7.3: Student Prevention Plan

Below are questions you will need to think about and complete before you begin your plan in Parent/Student Activity 7.1. Review the following questions, then complete the plan together. Make sure you put a copy in your suitcase!

1. What is the hardest part of living with your issue/concern/condition?
2. What has worked in the past to reduce the likelihood of increasing your symptoms?
3. Are there special medications, devices, or machines that are helpful? (Colleges can sometimes accommodate these for you.)
4. Who needs to know about your conditions at college?

PARENT/STUDENT ACTIVITY 7.1:

My Prevention Plan

My concerns are:

_____

My medications are:

_____

Any emergency procedures I may need to complete. Do I understand what
I need to do?

_____

_____

_____

What is the campus emergency number?

_____

College health center number and location:

_____

What is the easiest way to get there?

_____

Local pharmacy name and number:

_____

Primary Physician: name and phone number at college:

_____

Primary Physician: name and phone number at home:

_____

Physician specialists name/number:

_____

Physician specialists name/number:

_____

Nearest minute clinic name/number:

_____

What is the number and location of the closest Mental Health Crisis Line—on
and off campus?

_____

_____

What is the mental health warm line name/number? (If available, this is a hot
line that can be used to talk about concerns, but not necessarily a crisis)

_____

What are the numbers and locations for Rape Crisis and Emergency room?

_____

_____

What are the triggers that increase my illness or mental health conditions?

1. _____

2. _____

3. _____

4. _____

List the physical symptoms that I can identify when I need assistance to get additional help.

1. _____

2. _____

3. _____

4. _____

5. _____

How long will I wait until I contact home to inform them that my strategies are not working? _____

When do I call 911?

_____

What are the coping strategies I used in the past that were of some benefit?

1. _____

2. _____

3. _____

4. _____

Are they available at college? If so, where?

_____

Academic support center name/number

_____

Student disabilities center (504/IEP) name/number

_____

7.4: Additional Support

The process of identifying and setting up such a prevention plan can be tax-ing for both students and parents. Just thinking about something traumatic happening can be gut-wrenching. If it seems like both of you are not making progress with the plan, it may be time to seek the help of a professional. It is very common for seniors to meet with a therapist to discuss issues and receive support to create a functional and effective plan for transitioning to college. Meeting with the school counselor could also be helpful. Counselors or therapists can start the planning process and, after it is developed, bring in parents to get their feedback and hear the objectives the plan will achieve. Parents have reported to us that creating a prevention plan was constructive and that the counselor/therapist said exactly what they would have said to their student. Meeting with the counselor/therapist served to reinforce the need for the student to protect and care for themselves. In addition, mental health professionals can provide your family with many resources for all kinds of mental health centers and community supports.

VOICES FROM CAMPUS 7.1

Emily

Emily returned from her first year of college very appreciative of all the time spent on the college transition plan that she set up with her family and school counselor. She described having a bit of a rough start to her fall semester, but because she had a list of contacts, she could set up appointments early on. Emily's roommate was not that lucky, however. Emily believed she struggled with a mental health issue and really did not have any kind of support in place. Emily's roommate kept saying she thought things were going to get better for her, but Emily could tell she wasn't eating enough or socializing with others. Her roommate continued to get further behind in schoolwork and had difficulty getting out of bed in the morning, which meant she missed many of her early classes. Emily decided to speak with their resident advisor (RA) confidentially to let her know that she was concerned and worried about her roommate's well-being. The RA spoke with the student, and at first it seemed to help, but shortly after things got worse. Emily's roommate failed three of her five classes her first semester. She was put on academic probation for the next semester. The roommate and her family made the decision to drop out of the university to seek other options. Emily received a new roommate for the second semester, and later learned that the former roommate, after taking the second semester off, enrolled in a local community college closer to home.

7.5: The Take Away

We hope that you take the following away from this chapter:

- With proper planning, students with medical and/or mental health conditions can be successful in college.
- Creating a prevention plan will provide a sense of reassurance and empowerment, and will reduce stress levels.
- Developing written protocols for mental and physical health concerns are important for overall health in college, and beyond.

7.6: References

Center for Disease Control (CDC). 2014. Ten leading causes of death by age group. Retrieved from https://www.cdc.gov/injury/images/lccharts/leading_causes_of_death_age_group_2014_1050w760h.gif

DRUGS, ALCOHOL, AND OTHER RISKY BEHAVIORS

Reading the title of this chapter you may be tempted to skip it if you feel it doesn't apply to you and your student. However, we feel it is one of the most important chapters, especially given the sad reality that all of us will be touched in some way by the negative effects of drugs, alcohol, and other forms of risky behavior. As parents, we never want to believe that something bad could happen to our children, and imagining something bad happening could cause some to enter into a state of panic. The National Institute on Alcohol Abuse and Alcoholism on January 15, 2015, reported that approximately 1,800 students die every year from alcohol poisoning, 600,000 are injured while intoxicated, and nearly 100,000 students become victims of an alcohol-influenced sexual assault. The truth is, when they go off to college, your student will be exposed to many things outside of yours and their control, and it is important they are provided with the necessary survival techniques as they navigate their new college environment. Your senior is about to be totally responsible for their own safety and well-being and will have to manage the unlimited options for their free time. Just consider the experience of one of our students, Lauren (see Voices From Campus 8.1).

VOICES FROM CAMPUS 8.1

Lauren

Lauren stopped by the high school counseling center after her freshman year of college. She told us about what a great and enriching experience she had and that she plans to return in the fall. She reported that the only scary thing that happened to her was an incident with her roommate on her second day of orientation. They were deciding what to do for the weekend, and her roommate asked if she was going to attend the university-sponsored dance on campus for new students. Lauren told her that she would go with her. The dance was really fun! Lauren saw lots of new faces and there were a lot of faculty present. Lauren also met a bunch of other students who were living in her dorm, and she recognized some students from her high school.

Lauren met a nice upperclassman who invited her to another party right after the dance. He said that the party was super easy to find and lots of other students were coming from the dance. This was exciting to Lauren. She felt like the year was off to a great start. Lauren asked her roommate if she was going with her, but the roommate said she was starting to get a cold and really needed to sleep. Lauren decided to go to the party anyway because it was so close to campus. She found the house easily (there were lots of other students hanging out on the porch). Lauren went in to look around and see if there was anyone that she knew. As soon as she entered the door some guy came up to her and handed her a drink. Everyone seemed so pleasant. Then the upperclassman from the dance spotted her, said hello, and asked if she wanted a tour of the house. Lauren agreed. All the rooms had loads of students in them and it seemed like everyone was having a great time. When they both arrived at his bedroom there were about seven other students in there. The guy asked her if she wanted to try a really awesome drink they were serving. Lauren sensed he was being pushy and trying to get her to drink, but she tried it anyway because she thought that he was just being hospitable. They said that the drink had to be guzzled all at once, not sipped like a baby. As Lauren put her head back to drink the shot, everyone slowly left the room. And then all the lights went out in the room and she was in the complete dark. Lauren quickly grabbed her jacket that had her phone and keys in it. The guy she met at the dance was the only other person left in the room. He moved close to Lauren and tried to get her to kiss him. She said no and asked how to get out of the room. She got up and started feeling for the door. The upperclassman came at her again, shoved her on the bed, and tore at her shirt. Lauren, shocked, was caught off guard and didn't know what to do. There was a long battle, with the upperclassman attempting to force himself on her. Lauren finally grabbed her jacket again and pushed the guy away from her as hard as she could. He fell to the ground. Lauren then found the door, but she struggled to open it because it was locked. She was finally able to get out of the room and ran out of the house. She ran all the way back to her dorm. Lauren's heart was pounding as she entered her room. She did not know what to do next. She was not sure if the upperclassman was coming after her or not. She thought she may have hurt her arm in the struggle. As Lauren told her roommate what had happened, she felt embarrassed and realized she was set up by the upperclassman from the moment he met her at the campus party. Lauren started to think about what could have happened if she was not able to escape the bedroom. This incident left her very upset and at a loss as to who to go to for support.

Lauren shared that she has learned many lessons as a result of that night. She feels very lucky things did not get worse. She really felt like she never had to worry about these kinds of things before now. She realized she needed to be more conscious about her own safety.

Students who have thought about challenging situations are better prepared to recognize potential risky behavior and know what to do and what not to do in certain situations. The simplest form of such awareness is in the recognition that there are specifics times and even circumstances in which the risk is elevated. As their school week comes to an end and the allure of the upcoming weekend is drawing closer, being prepared and thinking about actions and personal safety before they participate in an adventure should be first and foremost in their minds.

8.1: Alcohol Use and Alcohol Poisoning

As noted above, the sad reality is that students are injured and die from alcohol misuse and abuse. Too often our young adults, and possibly ourselves, view the use of alcohol as benign or as a social activity. Take a moment and review the following "Did You Know?" quiz. Which of the following did you know? It would be helpful to discuss this quiz with your student.

Did You Know?

1. The following are symptoms of alcohol poisoning:

   A. Vomiting, quick breathing, passing out

   B. Vomiting, drop in body temperature, slow breathing, pale skin

   C. Vomiting, high body temperature, passing out

   Did you choose B? That is correct. Also, besides vomiting, slow breathing, and pale skin, other signs could be confusion, seizures, or has passed out and cannot be awakened. It is not necessary for the person to experience all of these symptoms in order to seek help. Students often dismiss these symptoms and let the student "sleep it off" only to find out they never woke up.

2. Which of the following is defined as "one alcohol drink?"

   A. 20 ounces of beer or 8 ounces of wine or 2 ounces of hard liquor

   B. 3 ounces of beer or 4 ounces of wine or 2 ounces of hard liquor

   C. 12 ounces of beer or 5 ounces of wine or 1.5 ounces of hard liquor

Did you choose C? This is correct. It is important to allow your body time to get rid of the alcohol in your system. The more one drinks in a short amount of time, the greater risk of alcohol poisoning. If you have one drink, you should then give yourself one hour for your body to successfully disperse it.

3. What are risk factors for alcohol poisoning?

    A. Your size and weight

    B. Your tolerance level

    C. Whether you have eaten recently

    D. All of the above

D is correct. A wide range of factors increase your risk of alcohol poisoning.

4. Since binge drinking is a major cause of alcohol poisoning, how much alcohol consumption would be considered binge drinking?

    A. Four drinks in two hours for females; five for males

    B. Six drinks in one hour for males; four for females

    C. Eight drinks in two hours for both

If you chose A, you are correct. It only takes four drinks in two hours for a female to be considered binge drinking, and five drinks in two hours for males.

5. Ninety percent of binge drinkers, that experience alcohol poisoning, were dependent on alcohol? True or false?

The answer is false. Most students were not dependent alcohol drinkers. Most students are not experienced with alcohol use.

6. Providing food or coffee can help the person sober up and reduce the likelihood of alcohol poisoning. True or false?

False. The only way for a student to become sober is with time. Providing food and coffee could increase the possibility of them vomiting or choking. Students need to understand the risks involved with alcohol use. This is especially important because drinking is so ingrained in our culture and is an unofficially accepted part of the college experience. Most campuses are very concerned about the amount of underage drinking that occurs and have set up systems to reduce the use and misuse of alcohol. It is important to review your student's college's discipline guidelines for students both on and off campus. Some colleges will not tolerate more than one case of underage drinking. If a student is asked to leave school due to a major discipline issue, they may lose both college credits and financial aid.

We all know from personal experience or from watching television and movies what it looks like when someone has had a little too much to drink. Many students have asked us, "How can I tell when someone who is drinking has entered into alcohol poisoning?" The answer is not an easy one, because both intoxication and alcohol poisoning can appear to be similar. While this is a concern, we believe that it is not one raised to the level of life and death as it should be. The news has certainly noted the dangers of alcohol, just look at the injury and deaths reported on college campuses recently. So it is important for us to understand the signs of alcohol poisoning and have a clear idea of what it means when someone is intoxicated to a life-threatening degree. To be on the safe side, if at any time a student is unable to respond, confused, unable to talk, or has difficulty staying awake, you should be concerned. If the person becomes sweaty or pale, it is even more concerning. Students: If you are with someone when this happens, for their own safety, don't leave them alone! If you think a person may be experiencing alcohol poisoning, get medical help immediately. You may have to call 911 if their condition gets worse. Get them to respond to you in order to keep them alert (ask them questions, get them to answer) as you are trying to reduce the possibility of them slipping into a coma. It is important to turn the person on their side so that if they vomit, it can be expelled from their mouth instead of choking on it. Keep a close eye on their breathing. If they stop breathing, you may have to perform CPR or find someone that is trained to do so.

8.2: Drug Abuse

Currently the biggest problem regarding drug use is the abuse of pain killers, particularly opioids, and the use of heroin. Opioid and heroin use has been on the rise in recent years in the United States, and as a result, the death toll has risen accordingly. The annual death rate for drug overdoses is higher than for those who die from vehicle accidents. According to the Centers for Disease Control, the death rate from drug overdoses averages 110 per day, and more than half of those involve opioids. The death rate nationally has increased for adults ages 18-22. A large percentage of those deaths in this age range were due to patients being introduced to painkillers after a surgery. When we typically think about the use of painkillers we assume that it is for a major surgery or orthopedic injury. While these are certainly circumstances that may introduce a student to painkillers, that introduction could come as a result of something as common as having a wisdom tooth extracted. In the past, when a person got their wisdom teeth extracted, they were prescribed 30 painkillers by a doctor, when only 5 may have been necessary. In our experience, when talking with students who have become addicted, they typically say that if the doctor is prescribing the pills to them then it means they must not be bad for you. What students don't realize is just how similar these painkillers are to heroin. Both are opioids which attach to specific molecules, referred to as opioid receptors. They decrease feelings of pain and make people feel so relaxed and happy that they are unaware of the damaging effects. For some students it only takes a short amount of time before they are dependent on the drugs. When the money runs low to purchase painkillers they often turn to heroin, which is a cheaper drug with a much better "high." Many of our students have reported to us that other students have approached them after a surgery asking for their leftover medications. At just one of the high schools in our school district, there have been 11 deaths from overdoses. The students were in their early to mid-twenties, making many of them college-age. It is important not to dismiss this data. Our district is like so many other suburban districts across the country. The use of prescription pain medications across our nation's high schools and colleges is truly an epidemic that requires our attention and care to deal with it effectively.

8.3: What to Do

If you are aware that your student struggles with drugs or alcohol misuse and abuse, it is important to secure resources ahead of time. Locating treatment facilities as well as Alcoholics Anonymous (AA) and Narcotics Anonymous (NA) meetings will be vital to your student's success and will help prevent relapse (see the additional resources at the end of this chapter).

Once on campus, it is important for your student to know the location of the college's counseling center. These centers are available to students and many of them have certified addictions counselors. Setting up an appointment to meet with the staff and get familiar with the location and services provided could be beneficial. It has been increasingly popular to provide sober living dorms and recovery programs on college campuses. For students that do not want to tempt themselves by the constant exposure to alcohol and drugs, this is an excellent option. For the latest information on drug use among teenagers, visit the National Institute for Drug Abuse website: https://teens.drugabuse.gov/. For more information about sober dorms and recovery programs, visit https://www.quitalcohol.com/sobriety/sober-living-in-universities.html/.

8.4: Environmental Risks

Most college campuses are safe places for students. Almost all of them have well-established security staff and systems in place for rapid responses to crises and threats. Text alerts are now sent to students when there are concerns. However, some campuses are surrounded by areas that are not nearly as safe. If your student prefers staying on campus and never straying from it, then it shouldn't be a problem. But if your student enjoys a nightlife off-campus, a little more investigation is needed.

Colleges report their crime rates annually, but they are only campus statistics. As a parent, you may want to research the areas surrounding the campus to get an accurate picture of how safe the area is. If you are having difficulty locating crime statistics, we have directed parents to call the local police station where the college resides. They can offer you plenty of information along with advice on which extra safety precautions you need. We are not trying to dissuade students from attending schools located around high crime areas, but we do advise that every student is prepared and aware of their surroundings. Many of our students who attend city universities have incredibly enriching experiences. This is in part because they learned very early on which areas were safe to go into and which to avoid . . . especially when walking alone. Seniors, we recommend talking with current college students when you visit campus, attend orientation day, placement testing, or an open house. Any input will put you in a safer position once the school year starts.

8.5: Date Rape

Date rape (or acquaintance rape) happens on every college campus. The combination of additional freedom, a desire to explore sexually, coupled with alcohol and/or drug-inhibited decision-making make for a risky combination. More than 50 percent of the sexual assaults happen on college campuses involve students under the influence of alcohol. Students report to us that there are specific parties set up to take advantage of freshmen sexually, usually after the introduction of shots of alcohol and beer.

It is perfectly understandable that your future college student will want to attend parties. A simple but effective strategy is to use the *buddy rule*. This rule is simply a commitment to attend parties with a friend, one from whom you won't separate. Make a safety pledge to make plans with your buddy before going anywhere. Have a signal or safe word prepared to alert each other that the other person is uncomfortable and ready to leave. This is why it is so important to meet and make friends early in the fall semester, or even during orientation. If they have a cup in their hand, they should never set it down. Tranquilizer drugs such as rohypnol ("roofies") and ketamine, just to name a few, can be put into drinks without even causing a difference in taste. This allows the person doing the drugging to lure the student into doing anything without a struggle.

If a student is involved in a situation and they are not sure what to do or not comfortable with contacting community resources, encourage them to speak with their resident assistant (RA). Most RA's are trained to direct students to the appropriate resources.

While college life is and should be fun and exciting, it is also, like everything in life, something that should be approached with a sense of self-preservation. The following are a number of simple yet effective safety tips to consider.

8.6: The Take Away

We hope that you take the following away from this chapter:

- Understanding the risk factors of alcohol and drug use is critical to personal safety.

- Preparing for possible traumatic situations, such as sexual assault or alcohol/drug overdoses, could ensure reduced reaction time for the student and their friend, and speed up the securing of appropriate resources as quickly as possible.

- Knowing your college campus and your surrounding community will help to ensure that you are safe at all times.

8.7: References

National Institute on Alcohol Abuse and Alcoholism. (December 2015). *College drinking.* Retrieved from https://pubs.niaaa.nih.gov/publications/collegefactsheet/Collegefactsheet.pdf

Centers for Disease Control and Prevention. (December 30, 2016). *Increases in drug and opioid-involved overdose deaths—United States, 2010–2015.* Retrieved from https://www.cdc.gov/mmwr/volumes/65/wr/mm655051e1.htm?utm_campaign=colorado.ourcommunitynow.com%20website&utm_source=ocn_story&utm_medium=website

8.7: List of Recovery Websites

Alcoholics Anonymous – www.aa.org

Narcotics Anonymous – www.na.org

https://www.addictionsandrecovery.org has an excellent list of recovery websites

8.8: SAMHSA Hotline

The Substance Abuse and Mental Health Services Administration (SAMHSA) has a National Helpline that is a free, confidential, 24/7, 365-day-a-year treatment referral and information service (in English and Spanish) for individuals and families facing mental and/or substance use disorders.

LEAVING HOME

Dear High School Graduate (or future graduate if you are reading this early),

Your high school principal has just handed you your high school diploma. Congratulations! The future is in your hands! Now—what's next???

You have also completed Chapters 1 through 8—so good for you! Now, the real work begins.

It is time to leave your family home and begin your college adventure! You have already navigated through many significant moments this year: homecoming, senior prom, and most importantly, the "Big G"—graduation! Goodbyes have been made to your teachers and friends (don't worry, you can keep in touch via Snapchat and Instagram or maybe even visit them in college, but more on that later), and you have attended your last graduation party. But as you slowly start to notice those oh-so-familiar back-to-school ads that creep into our televisions and newspapers every summer, those small, but painful, reminders make you realize your summer of freedom will soon give way to the mundane reality of school. Only this time it will be *different*, because you are going off to college!

In this chapter, we will explore ways to prepare for the journey from your family home into your new college digs. We will also discuss ways to stay in communication with your family and friends as well as how to navigate successfully inside and outside of your college environment.

9.1: Gather Your Belongings

You may think: "I know what I need to bring. I don't need to make a list for college." However, the earlier in the summer that you begin to organize, the less likely you are to forget something important that you only remember once you're settled into your new room and start looking for it. We feel it is very important that you first create a list of personal, must-have-with-you items—those that you feel absolutely, positively must be on campus with you and cannot stay at home. Using the sample Want/Need List (see Your Turn 9.1) as a guide, construct your own list to guide your packing process. While completing the list, keep in mind how you will be getting to school (car, airplane, train, bus, helicopter, etc.) and if that mode of transportation will be able to accommodate all of the items on your list.

YOUR TURN 9.1

Want/Need List

Item	Need with Me	Want with Me	Can Stay Home
Cell phone			
Laptop/computer/tablet			
Headphones			

Item	Need with Me	Want with Me	Can Stay Home
Steaming media device			
TV			
Gaming consoles			
DVD player			
Designer clothes			
Magazines			
Photo album			
Favorite shoes/sneakers			
Favorite games/toys/etc.			
Sporting equipment (volleyball, tennis racket, basketball, etc.)			
Coats, jackets, etc.			
_____			
_____			
_____			
_____			

The interesting part about completing that want/need checklist is that if you chose the "Want with Me" column instead of the "Need with Me" one, chances are that the wanted items will probably not affect your life drastically if you decide to leave them at home. Don't worry, unless your parents decide to turn your room into a walk-in closet while you are away, the left-behind items will be right where you left them (you should probably clear this with them first)! This list may be influenced not only by your mode of transportation to and from college, but also by the number of times that you are able to go home over the course of the school year. For example, if you know that you are going home for winter break, you probably don't need to bring your snowboard with you in August!

In addition to the want/need list, there are other necessary items that you may not think about too often because you have easy access to them at home. Our advice is to get these items together in advance during the summer while you are at home instead of scrambling to find things in your campus community, where many of your future classmates will be doing the same thing. The following checklist (see Your Turn 9.2) was adapted from the West Chester University of Pennsylvania's (2017) Office of Residence Life and Housing Services website. The list contains many items that may be off your radar to bring because they were always in your bathroom's medicine cabinet or linen closet waiting for you. Use this list as a guide and, like before, review with your parents and check off the things that you will need to purchase for your new living quarters.

YOUR TURN 9.2

What to Bring

Bedding
- Sheets (know your bed size)
- Blanket
- Pillow
- Comforter/Bedspread
- Bed Skirt
- Mattress Cover, Mattress Pad, or Featherbed

Appliances
- Refrigerator (no larger than 3.6 cubic ft.)*
- Microwave (no larger than 0.7 cubic feet permitted)*
- TV/DVD/MP3/iHome/Stereo*
- Vacuum*

Laundry Items
- Laundry Bag/Basket
- Detergent
- Fabric Softener
- Quarters

Miscellaneous Items
- Hangers
- Lanyard/Key Ring
- Deck of Cards
- Stationery
- Postage Stamps
- Paper Products (napkins, towels, plates)
- Plastic Goods (forks, cups, bowls)
- Food Storage Containers
- Movies
- Carpet and/or Area Rug*
- School Supplies (disks, stapler, etc.)
- Coaxial Cable or HDMI Cable
- Sewing Kit
- Umbrella
- Flashlight
- Cleaning Supplies

Room Accessories
- Alarm Clock with Battery Backup
- Lamp* (no halogen lamp)
- Storage Crates/Bins
- Fan*
- Audio Entertainment Devices

- Decorations (posters, pictures, etc.)
- Computer

Toiletries
- Towels
- Washcloths
- Shower Caddy
- Shower Shoes (flip flops, etc.)
- Robe
- Shampoo, Conditioner
- Soap
- Hair Products
- Toothbrush/Toothpaste

First Aid
- Band-Aids
- Antibiotic Cream
- Tylenol, Advil
- Cold Medicine
- Any Prescribed Medications

What Not to Bring
- Appliances of any kinds with an exposed heating element, including but not limited to hot plates, toaster ovens, deep fryers, electric frying pans, sandwich makers, grills (like the George Foreman Grill), halogen lamps, are not permitted in any housing facility.
- Heavy appliances are prohibited.
- Candles and incense are not allowed in any housing facility.
- Octopus plugs of any kind, and extension cords/power strips that do not use Fire Shield technology.
- Window air conditioners
- Pets (including fish)

- Lofts
- Water beds/aquariums (or any large water holding device)
- Street signs or neon signs

*: You should contact your roommate(s) first before bringing these items. You may not want/need two of them!

Source: Adapted from West Chester University of Pennsylvania's Office of Residence Life and Housing Services, 2017.

9.2: Move-In Day

A popular tradition among new college students is freshman move-in day, where new students arrive with their parents who help them get settled in to their new living situation. While you may think the idea of your parents, aunts/ uncles, siblings, cousins, or family friends helping pack and carry boxes and luggage into your room with you is embarrassing, think about how you might feel if they *didn't* come with you. Move-in day can be very stressful, and the more help and support that you have, the better! Carl (Voices From Campus 9.1) shared what happened when he endured move-in day by himself.

VOICES FROM CAMPUS 9.1

Carl

I was so happy to leave home and go to college! I love my parents, but I couldn't wait to graduate and head off on my own. My parents asked me if I wanted help moving in to my dorm, but being the proud person that I was, I said "no, but thank you anyway," and started to plan my move. On move-in day, which was the Saturday before classes started, I work up early, packed my car, hugged and kissed my parents goodbye, and took off in my car for school.

When I got to my college, the campus was loaded with pick-up trucks, U-Hauls, and minivans, and my dorm was crowded with students and their families. I noticed parents and other family members all helping their sons and daughters move their belongings into their rooms. I admit I was kind of envious that they had help and I didn't. I ended up making *10* trips back and forth from my car to my new room, without anyone's help. Toward the end of the day, my new roommates and their family members saw me struggling and offered to carry some of the things upstairs for me. I graciously accepted their offer. By this time I was beyond exhausted, and the experience helped me to learn a valuable lesson: if someone offers you help, especially during move-in day, and especially your *family*, don't turn them down! Not only is help nice, but the bonding I witnessed over the course of the day between all of the families was genuine and priceless. Next year, if my family is willing, I am going to ask for their help on move-in day!

As for how to survive move-in day itself, here are some suggestions for both parents and students to use. Review, and determine which ones work best for you!

Getting your belongings to campus. The most important thing to figure out before your move is if everything that you want to bring will fit in the space that you have. If you are driving to college, will all your belongings fit in your car? Do need a rental van? If you are flying, how many bags will you have to carry on the plane to bring everything that you want or need? Not to mention that there are typically limits as to how many bags you can take on a flight with you, and the excess baggage fees that come with them are not fun at all. It may prove to be cheaper and more efficient to ship your bulkier items to college by mail ahead of time to avoid these issues.

Students, if you want or need new things for your dorm room, try using online registries. Like wedding registries, Amazon, Target, and Bed, Bath & Beyond all have online services where you can create wish lists and buy items for your room (or have friends and family purchase them for you!) and have them sent directly to your college. With the craziness that goes on after high school graduation, this could be a great time-saver and one less thing to worry about.

Pre-move preparation. Sometimes, it's the little things that can make you the most stressed out on move-in day. The more you can learn in advance about what to expect, the better! Check your college website to see what they suggest you do before moving in. For example, you may need a school ID card to get into your building, or even your room, making getting this ahead of time a must. Also, your college may have information on moving services (college volunteers, local rental services) and what to bring/what not to bring that will save you time and energy needed for your move. Checking the layout of the campus and your residence hall is vital as well. Is there a parking lot near your dorm? Are there elevators, and how many? The logistics of getting things to your room may influence your plan of action as you start to pack your belongings.

Your packing plan should also be well thought-out. Buy any boxes and packing necessities before you leave. Any bedding or sheets can go in large garbage bags, easily accessible as soon as your get to your room. Anything that you don't want to get wrinkled should go on a hanger and covered in a garment bag (a large trash bag will work as well). Clothes that you'll need immediately, as well as mandatory toiletries and medications should be placed in a duffel bag so you have quick access to them (this is also good practice for when you go on weekend visits home or to visit your friends). Any additional medicinal or health and beauty products should be tightly secured so they don't break or open during your travels. This also pertains to your electronic devices, pictures, or any other fragile items that you are bringing with you. Seasonal clothing that you will need throughout the year, like sweaters and coats, can be placed in storage containers until it's time to use them.

The move-in day experience. Prepare yourself for a long day! It is definitely a good idea to check the weather in advance of the move to make sure your clothing will be appropriate for the conditions. Speaking of clothing – don't wear brand new clothes on move-in day - prepare to get dirty! We say this because there will be boxes, bags, and packing material everywhere since there will be dozens of students moving in at the same time you are that are probably going to drop and spill things everywhere. Also, your room itself might not be the spotless if the previous occupant didn't do a respectable job of making sure it was cleaned thoroughly. Which brings us to another point – bring cleaning wipes, gloves, and other household supplies to wipe everything down before you place your food / clothing /body on it. Wear comfortable clothes that you don't mind getting messed up. Additionally, bringing food and drinks along on the trip is not only good for your family, but also the student volunteers that may help you.

We recommend only immediate family go with you on move-in day – save the extended family trips for later on in the semester.

Get your room the way you want it. Students, let your parents help you one last time before they leave. This may mean they make your bed, stock your refrigerator, and organize your dresser drawers for you (if they don't, remember – underwear and socks go in the top drawers, sweatshirts and sweaters on the bottom!) The rest will be up to you! Unpack and organize everything you need as soon as possible (but after your family leaves) so you can rest and relax later. There is no reason to have unpacked boxes still in your room once classes start! Keep the cleaning materials, you'll need them. Ask your parents to take any extra items that you have decided you won't need back with them.

Saying goodbye. Parents and students, think about how you want to say goodbye to each other in advance. Move-in day arrives before you realize it, and then it is over. Take time to appreciate the moments that lead up to this day. Having a meal together as a family before you leave (or on the way to the college) can help create a lasting memory before the chaos of move-in day begins. Parents – leaving a note for your student to find and read later with words of love and support could do wonders for them (and you) as they begin they school year. Finally, pick a time to say goodbye, stick to it, and leave quickly, so you can give your student the space they need to spread their wings.

Move-in day is the last opportunity that parents and students have to be together. Sharing this experience with one another is a guaranteed way to create new memories and make a stressful day endurable, as well as unforgettable.

Students: Move-in day is the last opportunity that you have with your family before your whole life (and theirs) changes. Sharing the move-in experience with them is a guaranteed way to create new memories and make a stressful day bearable.

9.3: Setting Up a Communication/ Support System

Students: Once you get settled into your new room and the academic year begins, you will be flooded with new experiences, both good and bad. There may be some conflict between you wanting to take care of yourself completely without anyone's help and you feeling like you are "giving in" by asking for assistance. Sometimes, you may need a familiar voice to calm you down and offer sound advice. The comforting sound of a parent's voice, even when they drove you crazy when you lived with them full-time, can help calm you when you are upset or just reassure you that everything will be okay when everything feels like it's falling apart. A parent's love is unconditional, and they would much rather hear from you no matter what shape you are in than not at all.

So to reiterate: Call your parents, especially when:

- you are happy
- you are sad
- you are excited
- you feel like you are being left out or not connecting
- you get a good grade on your first midterm
- you decide to join a sorority or fraternity
- you meet that special someone
- you break up with that special someone
- you're sick
- you miss them
- it's their birthday or anniversary or special day

And for many more reasons, especially when you just want to say hello!

VOICES FROM CAMPUS 9.2

Sandra
FaceTime with Dad

I can't even begin to tell you the number times that I complained to my counselor about my dad during senior year. He constantly bothered me about finishing my college applications, applying for scholarships, and keeping my senior year grades up. I thought I would lose my mind! And if I forgot to make my bed or clean my room, he would say, "No one's going to want to have you as a roommate in college!" Now that I'm in college, and basically on my own, I keep hearing my dad's voice when it's time to study, or when my room gets messy, or if I'm just procrastinating on something. Now I kind of miss him. I know it's silly, but I FaceTime him at least twice a week just to see his face and hear those same words of wisdom that I used to ignore. I see now that he only wanted me to do well, and when I look at how some of my friends are doing this semester, I'm glad that my dad pushed me to be more responsible!

9.4: Visiting Other Friends

One of the benefits of being a high school graduate is that you now have friends attending college in lots of places. Taking a weekend (preferably one when a major test isn't due on Monday) to visit those friends is an enjoyable way to reconnect with them and experience a campus environment different than your own. It is also a way to recharge your batteries if the stress of the semester is getting to you. Hopefully, the visit will motivate you to stay committed and focused on school for the rest of the semester. Our recommendation is to visit during a major event (family and friends weekend, concert, sports game, home-coming, etc.) so you can have a blast or, if you just want quality time with your friend, visit during a quiet weekend (no major events happening) so you can just relax and catch up on how much your lives have changed. Make sure to talk with your friend beforehand about what you should bring (clothing, money, bedding, etc.) and which mode of transportation they recommend that you take. Trips to visit your friends will help reinforce your relationships with them as you go through college, and it will also make you more self-sufficient by planning the excursion and traveling to other college campuses.

VOICES FROM CAMPUS 9.3

Jennifer

Homecoming Weekend

This year, I went to *two* homecomings! One was at my college, and the other was at Dana's college in Washington, D.C. I took the train there, which was a fun but scary experience because I never took the train before and didn't know what I was doing. But Dana gave me a train schedule and directions, so it wasn't too bad!

Dana's campus was amazing! I saw many similarities to my campus. They have a large dining hall like mine, and the rooms were sort of similar, but the energy was different. I guess it was because they are located in the city; things just seemed to move faster than my college in the middle of nowhere. But their homecoming was *crazy*! Dana and I went to the homecoming concert, and suddenly, out of the blue, Beyoncé showed up! She made a surprise appearance, sang a couple of songs for us, and then left in a helicopter. That was an experience that would never have happened at my school. I am so glad that Dana invited me to visit and that I was able to share such a fun weekend with her. I can't wait until next year!

9.5: Conclusion

Dreams of going to college and physically getting there are two different things. Your high school graduation should involve a period of celebration with friends and family, but after the parties are over and the glow of finally graduating from high school has faded, you should begin the task of preparing for your new life. Involve your parents in the planning and moving process! They will provide you with the extra insight and support that you need for your transition to go smoothly. Finally, just because you left home does not mean that you won't miss it occasionally, or the family and friends that you left there. Stay in regular communication with them, and planning a few face-to-face visits when you need a change of environment, or just that feeling of being loved and cared for that can only come from your family and friends, may be just what you need.

9.6: The Take Away

We hope that you take the following away from this chapter:

- It is very important to be as organized as possible when planning your move to college. Having both a *Want/Need* and *What to Bring* list is the best way to avoid leaving essential items at home.
- Include your family in the college move-in process. Their support will be wanted and needed on what will prove to be a very stressful and emotional day.
- Call your parents!
- Make time to schedule weekend visits to see your friends. Treat them like mini-vacations!

9.7: References

Grown and Flown. (2017). It's here: College move-in day. Retrieved from https://grownandflown.com/college-move-in-day/
West Chester University of Pennsylvania. (n.d.). What to bring. Retrieved from https://www.wcupa.edu/_services/stu.lif/whatToBring.aspx

IS THIS COLLEGE A GOOD FIT FOR ME?

The process of investigating colleges, preparing for SAT and ACT tests, and filling out endless amounts of paperwork all in hopes of gaining entrance to one's college of choice is exhausting. This process can also be frustrating when, once accepted and actually living on campus, you begin to question whether or not this college is actually the best fit for you.

As school counselors, we always see parents and students putting a great deal of time, money, and effort into SAT/ACT tutoring, AP testing, and dual enrollment programs for early college exposure. But in our experience, we feel that it is not the *academic* obstacles that challenge and frustrate students once they enter college, but it is the lack of preparation for the inevitable lifestyle change that occurs once college begins, and the lack of adaptability and resiliency skills that become evident and keep students from thriving on campus. This is especially problematic when a student cannot determine whether the source of their dissatisfaction is the fact that the college is simply not a good fit for them or the fact they lack the readiness necessary to make the most of out their college experience.

The solution for many students is to simply transfer out of the college and find a new one. And if that student does find themselves transferring to another school, the danger of repeating the same mistakes is high. That is why it is so important for you and your newly minted college freshman to review their experience and assess their social and emotional well-being during the first semester of college.

The first few months of college are expected to be somewhat stressful and even chaotic. It is truly a different world to which the new student is trying to adjust. However, the three to four week time period between semesters or even the Thanksgiving or winter break may provide the distance and time from campus necessary to reflect upon their fall semester. Through self-examination, students can go over different aspect of their college experience, and take note of those experiences that were stimulating and those that were draining, and develop a plan to address and resolve any issues inhibiting their growth and repeat positive experiences proven invaluable to their ongoing success. But all of this first starts with the student having an honest discussion with themselves.

10.1: Time to Take Stock

Yes, it is early in your student's college experience, but it's not too early to review, reflect, and adjust. The transition from youth into adulthood can be a rollercoaster of positive and negative experiences. It is normal for there to be several areas of concern or aspects of college life that could be the focus for adjustment. Let's look at Connor's experience as an example (Voices From Campus 10.1).

VOICES FROM CAMPUS 10.1

Connor
Making New Friends

Connor had a very difficult first few months of college. He found it very hard to make new friends. There were many nights where Connor sat alone in the cafeteria. Even after he saw people that he recognized from class or from his residence hall, he didn't make a move to sit with them. "I don't know what to say," Connor thought. "What if they think I'm stupid, or not chill?"

Connor came to the realization that he didn't like to make small talk with others. He wanted to *really* get to know someone, and not just talk about the weather, or some other trivial topic. Frustrated with his inability to strike up a conversation with the people in the cafeteria, Connor started to order take-out dinner from the student activities building and eat alone in his room.

One day, while exiting the activities building with his calzone and breadsticks, Connor noticed a flyer showing a person wearing a very familiar mask. The word "PAINTBALL" was in bold print at the top of the page. Connor, a huge paintball fan, used to play paintball all the time with his old high school friends. It turns out that there was a chapter of the National Collegiate Paintball Association (NCPA) right on campus! Connor thought that this was a sign. If he was ever going to make friends in his new school, it was going to be with people that may love paintball as much as he does. Connor put his food and drink on the closest table and took a picture of the meeting information with his phone.

It may be helpful for you, like Connor, to do some self-reflecting once you are on campus to assess how your semester is going. The questions found in Your Turn 10.1 provide a starting point for your reflection, discussion, and planning. The questions and subsequent discussion will give you a chance to examine each aspect of college life and target areas that are of concern. Reflecting on the initial college experience is crucial to understanding what has worked and what hasn't so far in the semester.

YOUR TURN 10.1

Taking Stock

Now that you almost have an entire semester under your belt, sit down with your parents, family member, or trusted friend to go over this list to self-assess your progress so far.

Question	All of the time	Some of the time	Never	Why or why not?
The college experience is what I expected.				
The adjustment to college was difficult without my family and friends around.				
I am happy with my academic progress.				
I am content with my physical health.				
I was able to get involved in college-related activities.				
I am aware of or have accessed my college academic resources.				
I am able to maintain a regular eating/sleeping schedule.				
I was able to find friends that I felt comfortable with this semester.				
My partying habits affected my ability to attend classes this semester.				
I was able to stay within my financial budget this semester.				
I was able to take care of my laundry and basic hygiene needs.				

Question	All of the time	Some of the time	Never	Why or why not?
I met and interacted with a person from a culture different than my own.				
I feel like I belong at my college, and I feel supported by most people there.				
I felt organized and prepared for all of my classes this semester.				
I am accessing or aware of off-campus resources (medical, entertainment, financial, etc.).				

10.2: A Plan of Adjustment

As noted above, hitting a few rough spots or feeling somewhat uncomfortable and stressed is to be expected when making such a big transition of going from the safe and familiar environment of home to college. So perhaps the first part of any plan for adjusting to challenges is to simply . . . take a breath. When feeling stressed one's tendency to run from the perceived source of that stress is not always the most efficient and beneficial way to handle it. It is important to slow down and recognize that things identified as problematic or concerning are in almost all cases resolvable.

The second step is to begin to create a plan to address and resolve any concerns identified in our initial reflection and discussion. Some of these things may feel unbearable or even unresolvable; however, if we take time to really assess what is going and what options are available, we will be able to answer the question "Now that I know what the problem is, what steps will I take to resolve it?"

Universities do not like to lose students. In most cases, while the problems you are experiencing may be new to you and them, it will not be new to the professionals on campus. The college or university has most likely developed mechanisms and resources to assist in these situations (see Voices From Campus 10.2).

VOICES FROM CAMPUS 10.2

Sara

That Wasn't as Hard as I Thought

Sara started her first semester in college on a strong note. Because she prepared well during her senior year of high school and in the summer before she left for college, Sara's transition was very smooth in respect to being prepared for class, joining activities, and managing her time wisely. However, it seems as if Sara's roommates and neighbors in her residence hall didn't have the same time management regimen as her. Whenever Sara tried to study after dinner, she became distracted by the level of noise coming from her suitemates. With the constant blasting of music, yelling and screaming in the common areas, and roommates either asking her stuff or talking excitedly to each other or on their phones, Sara came to the conclusion that her suite was not a suitable place for her to study. Frustrated, Sara went to her resident advisor (RA) Rachel and asked for advice. Rachel, in an understanding and supportive way, acknowledged Sara's feelings and shared that she went through the same thing during her freshman year. "Why do you think I became an RA?" Rachel laughed. "I have a room all to myself and get to study in peace and quiet!" Rachel then shared a "secret list" of locations around campus that were great for studying—places where she was able to get her work done in a quiet and secluded environment. Rachel also promised Sara that she would speak to the students on her floor at the next floor meeting about being considerate of roommates that may be studying around them.

The important thing when you are having difficulty with something is to seek out the right person to direct you to the best resource for the situation. Finding an effective solution and the correct resource may require some additional research, but it will be worth the time. Your resident advisor (RA) is a great person to start with, as well as your campus counseling center, your academic advisor, or even a class professor.

Personal initiative is required to benefit from all of the resources that are available to you. The staff on campus are there to help, but they are not in a position to rescue. You must speak up, and seek help. As such, the most important part of this plan is the development of your own voice and your ability to serve as your best advocate. Your *self-advocacy* is a vital part of the resolution process in every situation. If you never tell anyone that you are having problems, how will they know that you need help?

Review your responses to the questions you completed in Your Turn 10.1. Which areas did you find are in need of the most improvement? As you begin the process of planning to address these issues, concretely and specifically identify how you or your experiences will be different once these issues are rectified. It is important to be clear about the goal you are trying to achieve. As you reflect and discuss your goal, begin to identify what you can do differently to help you achieve your goal and which individuals or services might be helpful in your attempts to resolve the issue.

As with all planning, it is essential to be as concrete and specific as possible. Answer questions of "who," "when," "what," and "how" needs to be involved in resolving the concerns you have identified. For example, if you were not satisfied with your grades this semester, what can you do with the remaining time to improve them? You may want to visit your professor during office hours in order to get honest feedback on your performance. Or perhaps it would help to speak with a classmate who has As and ask how they did it, or even ask to see a paper or assignment. You don't have to do this all on your own. Who else should or could be involved? For example, you may find your campus academic center provides support and tips on improving organization, time management, and study skills, all of which may be helpful in addressing any concerns you may have about your current grades.

For any plan to be of use it needs to be specific and doable. Your Turn 10.2 offers a model for developing such a plan.

YOUR TURN 10.2 MAKING ADJUSTMENTS

Action Plan

Areas that need improvement	Steps you will take to improve in this area (make goals)	How will you measure your progress in each area?	When will you review your progress?
(Example): I do not feel prepared for my class.	Record assignments in advance for each class in my calendar/planner. Develop an organization system that works for me (folders/notebooks for each class). Schedule study time for each class, even when something is not due, to reinforce understanding of the material.	Number assignments completed by due date. Mid-year grades. End of semester grades.	Weekly

10.3: It's Not Me, It's the College!

Still not happy at your college?

If you have taken stock and developed a meaningful action plan and the areas of concern are not or cannot be resolved, then perhaps the problem is not simply "you" but a mix of you and this particular college experience. If, in doing the review, you find that most of the reasons you are not content really have to do with the actual college environment, then maybe a transfer to another school is warranted. We do caution you however, the adage "the grass is greener on the other side" does not always prove true. It has been our experience that it is better for those attempting to adjust to campus life to give it a full year (two semesters) to become fully acclimated to their new college setting and academic demands. Prior to simply bailing, be sure to take the Your Turn questions seriously and implement the action plan (see Voices From Campus 10.3).

VOICES FROM CAMPUS 10.3

Summer

Summer went back to visit her high school on the Tuesday before Thanksgiving break to get a copy of her transcript sent to a new college. While in the school's counseling office, Summer ran into her former school counselor. After pleasantries were shared, Summer explained that the school she went to just *wasn't for her* and that she filled out an application to transfer to the local community college. Her counselor asked her to elaborate on what she meant by that, and Summer explained further:

"Well, I thought the school was fun and all, I mean, I made some friends and I liked the professors and my classes, but I struggled to get things in on time, and my clothes just piled up, which made my roommate mad at me, and I didn't have enough money to do the things that I wanted to do. I'm going to live at home with my parents and go to the community college until I can figure things out."

As the discussion unfolded it became clear to the counselor that Summer's issues revolved around her ability to balance academics with her activities of daily living. The counselor was able to help Summer to reflect on her goals and how she envisioned college life. As a result of this process, the counselor was able to help Summer see that most of her stress and feelings of despair rested with her limited ability to manage her time and demands.

The counselor, with Summer's permission, called the Academic Support Center at the college together and they were able to find out that the center not only offered literature on time management and study skills but provided an ongoing support group for those struggling with this type of adjustment. The fact that other students were dealing with the same type of experience helped Summer feel less alone. Summer visited the Support Center after break, and the experience helped change her feelings about leaving college. She decided to finish out the semester before revisiting the idea of transferring to another school.

10.4: Planning on Leaving?

Even with honest reflection and excellent planning you may find the college wasn't what you expected or what you feel you want or need. That is okay. Research has shown that nearly 33 percent of undergraduate students transfer colleges at least once during their college experience (Leavitt, 2015). We just want to be sure that, should you decide to transfer, it is for the right reasons and will serve you well in the long run.

While it would not be unusual for you to feel so frustrated or disappointed that you stop showing up to your classes, this ultimately is not the best way to withdraw. It is important to speak with your academic advisor, who can then direct you to the best person, perhaps the department Chair, or Dean of Students, to help you withdraw from your school. You want to withdraw the correct way so that there are no financial obstacles in the way when it's time to enroll in another school. There could be lingering financial loose ends, such as outstanding tuition balances, pending reimbursements, or obligations with student loans that you may have resolve before you enroll into another college. For example, you will need to be sure that your bills are paid completely or the university will place a hold your academic records from your new school until all debts are resolved. It is important to know your college's policy for officially and effectively withdrawing, as well as the procedures that may need to be followed in order to have your records transferred to any new university or college. While we know that this is not a pleasant process, it must be handled appropriately to save you from headaches down the road.

The college experience can and should be an exciting and rewarding time for students. And while it is commonly assumed everything will be figured out once you set foot on campus, the truth is that often there are glitches and challenges to the adjustment process. Hopefully, after taking the time to step back, take a breath, review the specifics of those challenges, and, with the help of others, develop a plan to facilitate the adjustment, what started out as a rocky road will become a smooth path to your educational and vocational success.

10.5: The Take Away

We hope that you take the following away from this chapter:

- College, much like life, will be full of obstacles to overcome. Most of the time, this is part of adjusting to a new environment.

- Self-examination is important to help students figure out a plan to address and resolve any issues that impede their academic, social and emotional growth.

- Know your campus resources, such as your RA, academic advisor, learning center, counseling center, professors, and dean within your major.

- The decision to transfer to another school should be done after much self-reflection, consultation with family and college staff, and attempts to problem-solve your existing concerns.

10.6: References

Leavitt, Elly. (2015, July 15). Study: More than 33% of undergrads transfer college at least once. *USA Today*. Retrieved from http://college.usatoday. com/2015/07/15/one-third-of-undergrads-transfer-colleges/

www.ingramcontent.com/pod-product-compliance
Lightning Source LLC
Chambersburg PA
CBHW061753270326
41928CB00011B/2493